Weology

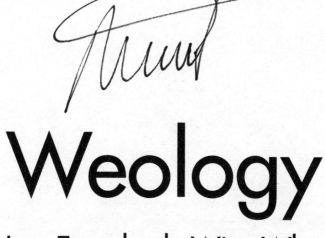

Weology

How Everybody Wins When We Comes Before Me

Peter Aceto
with Justin Kingsley

HarperCollins*Publishers*Ltd

Published by HarperCollins Publishers Ltd

First edition

HarperCollins books may be purchased for educational, business, or
sales promotional use through our Special Markets Department.

HarperCollins Publishers Ltd
2 Bloor Street East, 20th Floor
Toronto, Ontario, Canada
M4W 1A8

www.harpercollins.ca

Library and Archives Canada Cataloguing in Publication
information is available upon request.

ISBN 978-1-44342-950-4

Printed and bound in the United States of America
RRD 9 8 7 6 5 4 3 2 1

CONTENTS

The Humans   149

Conclusion: Click!

Ideas and Caffeine

Culture

Weology

AN INTRODUCTION TO WEOLOGY

I am not a banker.

Coming from the chief executive officer at one of Canada's biggest and most important financial institutions, this statement may come as a bit of a surprise. Finding out that I'm *not* a banker was certainly a shock to me.

It was a couple of months following a career move to the United States and a big promotion for me. My wife and I were at a house party organized by a colleague. I'd been with ING Direct for a number of years, but this was my first senior job. My "shot," as they say. I would be a top leader on the American lending team and working with a very accomplished lending expert. This was a good thing because I didn't know much about credit or lending. Everything I knew was related to *doing*. I was a doer, and now I'd be working for— and learning from—a very good credit expert. Made sense to me.

So, this was a Friday-night party with many work colleagues, their spouses and friends. A fellow named Jeffrey was there too, a close friend who had in many ways been a mentor to me. My wife and I were chatting with some friends at one end of the room, and my pal Jeffrey was at the other end, surrounded.

I can still see and hear him, holding court before a rapt audience, his big laugh booming and rebounding off the ceiling, people hanging from each syllable. Yet somehow I felt he was talking to me. He just had to be. His heavy, robust laughter was like an engine kicking into gear, a sound belonging to him and him alone. And I can still sense his gaze, the corners of his eyes spying for me as he spoke,

1

using long words and loud gestures. Like he was waiting to catch my glimpse, tug on the rod and reel me in.

Oh yes, I definitely remember the moment when he began screaming across the room at me:

"Hey, Peter! . . . Pete!"

I ignored him.

"Pete!"

Finally, I succumbed and turned slowly toward Jeffrey, and our eyes met.

"Hey, Pete, tell me, what are our mortgage rates?"

In the movie version of my life, the one that plays over and over in my head, the room fell silent when he asked me that question. The overheads dimmed. The spotlight caught me—pock!—my soles were glued to the floor and I was framed by a circle of light and floating flecks of dust, and there was nowhere to go, and it suddenly sucked being there. Necks craned in unison, people stopped mid sip, and curiosity was painted on the faces of all those assembled. Eyebrows arched. A look at the inside of their heads would reveal exactly what they must have been thinking: "What an odd question. Surely the man in charge of lending at a bank knows something as elementary as his own mortgage rates!"

I'm sure not one of them cared what our mortgage rates actually were, but they sure seemed interested in my answer.

The problem, as you've already guessed, is that I had absolutely *no idea* what our mortgage rates were. It had to be a setup. Jeffrey was well aware that I did not know what our rates were, as we'd discussed this many times. So what did I do, under the bright glare of the spotlight? I don't know for certain because I can't clearly remember the rest of what happened. I probably made a joke out of it, but the truth is that I only remember being seething mad. I was enraged and, worse, I couldn't show it. So I just deflected by saying something funny and took a very big sip of my drink.

For the rest of the interminable evening, I was upset that a peer would outrageously embarrass me this way. So publicly. So directly. And so insightfully!

Unable to get the thought out of my head, I made up scenarios. Maybe he was talking about how brilliant I was despite my lack of lending knowledge. Maybe he was telling a story about something unrelated, like helping a friend at the party who was buying a house. Maybe . . . but something in my heart made me confident that it wasn't the case.

As I let the anger simmer and stew, I altered my thinking but not for the better. I started thinking that maybe there was some resentment brewing about me.

CEO Arkadi Kuhlmann was a different kind of leader, and he had picked me for this job because he liked stray dogs. He built teams just like Major Reisman did in the *Dirty Dozen*: a ragtag bunch of misfits. His idea was that damaged people have lived through adversity and are therefore better suited to "getting things done" than anybody else—category experts included. How else could a neophyte lawyer be hired to work in a bank? And here I was, a decade younger than most of the executives, a new generation—and I didn't know the frigging mortgage rates.

My wife didn't say anything. No one said anything. I've never even discussed the episode with Jeffrey, who remains a friend. To this day I have no idea whether anybody except me remembers. Why? Because it was my fault. I should have known the darn rates, and from that day on for the rest of my life I vowed to learn from this lesson, this public spanking, and never let it happen again.

I thought: The next time I get asked that question I'd better know the answer, because it is a question to which I *should* know the answer. Preparedness doesn't just happen in the work setting—not when you're a leader or striving to become one.

The moral of this story is that, for my entire career I've been fighting against the fact that I'm in a leadership position but I've never been a subject matter expert. The way we are accustomed to thinking and reasoning builds certain expectations. People *expect* the head of a bank to fit their image of a banker—a slick-haired financial expert who uses the right words and numbers and wears pinstriped double-breasted suits.

Not me.

Some skills can be mastered by study, and numbers are only a question of recollection. One can say, "I don't know the mortgage rates, but I can learn to memorize them." That's easy. What matters to me is the desire and ability to learn as fast as possible. Other skills, like motivating people, can't be taught—they come from life experiences and the way they shape us as people. They come from *doing*.

The idea of *doing* is a recurring theme in this book, which also aims to be much more. I have tried to write a business book that is unlike other business books. Some will say it's not a business book at all, and that's just fine by me. As long as it's different and it moves something, anything, forward.

It bothers me when someone belittles others because of something he or she thinks they should know. I've developed the skill, the art, of getting up the learning curve faster than I need to. From what I remember, in my first job at a bank I was just trying to stay above water. That's why I don't feel like a pretender or a charlatan. It doesn't bother me that I'm not an expert—not like it did that fateful night.

I made a promise to myself after that party. I swore that I'd always, always, know our mortgage rates. And now that I'm CEO, as I sit here writing these lines, I realize that I don't have the slightest idea what our mortgage rates are at this moment. Why?

Because I am not a banker.

Where this book comes from

In 1975, Muhammad Ali was invited to address Harvard University's graduates at Senior Class Day. There were over 2,000 students in the room, most of them white-skinned apparently, to hear the GOAT (Greatest Of All Time) speak. There's a YouTube video featuring the writer George Plimpton, who explains what happened in the auditorium, but no footage from that day exists that I have been able to find.

At age 34, Ali was already a living legend. He was the undisputed heavyweight champion of the world, had changed from Cassius Clay to Muhammad Ali, refused to fight in Vietnam and had undergone imprisonment, had fought and defeated the "unbeatable" George Foreman in the "Rumble in the Jungle," and was entering the final stage of his fighting career. On top of everything, Ali was a fantastic poet. His nickname, before GOAT, was the Louisville Lip because he just always had something to say. "Your hands can't hit what your eyes can't see—I float like a butterfly, sting like a bee!"

When Ali started backing his words with action and results, he grew in stature and popularity.

It's important to note this because some people may think that Ali had always been a popular, iconic character—but that is not the case. By the mid-1970s, Ali's legacy was definitely growing, which is probably why he was invited to speak at Harvard.

And so the champ spoke. He used cue cards and explored all kinds of subjects, even dyslexia. He discussed the meaning of opportunity, chances he'd never had, and encouraged those present to forge their own paths through life based on their own strengths and advantages. When his speech was over, a lone voice rang out from the crowd. "Give us a poem!" one young man shouted.

Silence. All eyes were on the champ. And there, in that instant, in a flash of pure improvised genius, Ali composed what is recognized as the shortest poem ever recorded in the English language. He looked at those kids and said: "Me . . . We!"

Three letters organized into two little words. What a way to capture an era. The individual and the collective, one and the same. A new relationship between person and people. A unique way of boldly viewing how humanity can move forward. Fearlessness! In 1975, this poem carried a multitude of messages expressing the hopes of an entire generation. Ali nailed it.

We've seen many variations on the theme since Ali's brilliant invention.

When my co-author, Justin, and I discussed Ali's brilliant poem, we both felt we were on to something. We knew we had the roots of the idea for this book, that we could develop a concept that captured the essence of everything I've done as a business leader. We had, in four letters, the roots of a story that reaches back in time and stretches into the future.

What I'm trying to do as the leader of Tangerine is to build a culture in which individuals—people—have the means to truly thrive. To succeed. To be happy in their work. To feel fulfilled and growing. A culture that gives voice to all team members, no matter who they are or what they do. Why? Because being good to your own people is good business. When Me thrives, We benefit.

And so the title of this book is *Weology*. Its meaning is the thread that runs throughout and best expresses my own philosophy. What I call "Weology" is about creating win-win scenarios. It's transparency without asterisks. It's a way of putting people first in the short term so that a company can thrive in the long term. At first we called it

Wemeology, but we soon realized that the shorter, simpler term—Weology—did the job.

Of course, many of the initiatives we develop and implement don't immediately reflect growth on the bottom line, and that's okay. It's good. It's part of the plan. The calculation is that numbers don't have to rule the way a business—not even a bank—is run.

Here's one example of Weology thinking. I believe that the first 10 minutes of a meeting should actually be "wasted" chatting and catching up with people. *Hey, Brenda, how is your little crew doing? What are Walter and Rachel up to this summer? Did you go bowling last night?* Time-wasting and idle banter, yes, but only if you're counting beans for a living. From a human perspective, the significance is far greater. The message being sent is this: "We actually do care about you and your family and what's happening in your lives." This may seem trivial, which is actually the point. Trivial things make people feel good. It puts the spotlight on them and what, at first sight, appears to be mundane.

Where does the business factor in? Is this ad hoc niceness, or is there actually a system at work? Yes, in business there has to be. People who are happy in their work and feel valued will probably want to work with you for a longer time. They may want to spend extra hours finishing a project to ensure the company succeeds. They may decide that when they need professional change, they'd like to give it a try inside your organization, not outside for the competition. They will understand that when the We thrives, the Me wins too. Such people make the best kind of ambassadors for our company, our corporate culture, because they live Weology and know it's true.

Many companies make critical mistakes when they're trying to be good to their people. They say all the right words, but the proof fails to follow. Involvement delivers an experience, something a person can relate to, because living through an event means feeling emotion. Humans remember emotion. We recall the great times, and the sad ones too. We know that understanding is akin to empowerment. People who feel empowered become, in many ways, invincible.

Perhaps a better way to explain my goal might be to say that this is not a book about business, it's a book about need. What is need? What shape does it take? A great divide exists between "want" and "need," and this book is my attempt to convince people to focus a little more on their "needs" and a little less on their "wants."

To me, the pendulum is swinging too far toward the rich and too quickly away from the less well off. A few hundred years ago, people with golden crowns controlled commerce and money—everybody worked for the king. When the reins were loosened, in came elected governments and, more importantly, free economy. People started making their own money. They profited from their own business. As they got better at it, they amassed fortunes. But now the same system that empowered the masses is all too often supporting a rich few who are holding all the strings of power and control. This doesn't make any sense because I see an end to it. I see the eventual elimination of the middle class and the alienation of the poor, leading to revolt. What I'm trying to build in Tangerine's culture is a conscientious capitalism. A system that allows more individuals to benefit, to profit.

When Jeffrey called me out in front of colleagues, he was all Me and no We. He wasn't thinking about the impact it would have on me to be so embarrassed before my peers. Muhammad Ali's starting point, although he masked it with blustery quotes and bragging about his own greatness, has always been the We.

Together We (the collective) and Me (the individual) live and feed off one another, making Weology, hopefully, a roadmap for companies to follow.

The key, of course, is that We always comes first.

How this book was written

This book is founded on a collection of stories from my work and personal life, but it's not an autobiography. It's a book of ideas, of examples and suggestions that anyone can put into action. The way Justin Kingsley and I put these together starts with the stories, the recollections, because they prove that the ideas are more than theory. They're applicable. They've been put to the test. They've worked.

Over the course of many months in 2013, we started compiling these stories and lessons. We reviewed tens of thousands of words—from interviews, notebooks, blogs, tweets and any other material we could get our hands on—and chose what we hope are the best ones. Then we wove them into a collection based around the concept of Weology.

The structure of the book may seem unorthodox, but here is the thinking behind it. The three sections following this introduction make up the body of the work and best define my idea of Weology. It begins with "The Concept," which provides an overview of the vision. Next, "The Machine" explains the workings of the device that powers Weology. And finally, "The Humans" explores the key ingredient: you.

The next chapter, "Click," is the conclusion, but the book doesn't end there. It is followed by a section titled "Ideas and Caffeine," which is a selection of edited or rewritten blog entries that are closely connected to the idea of the book. I call them "Ideas and Caffeine" because that's often how I like to read—one or two short articles over a cup of coffee: a dose of caffeine and a shot of inspiration. These short bursts of inspiration, which are like poems to a guy like me, are excellent lessons to keep in mind.

I hope the insight into the philosophies that have shaped my approach to life and to business are instructive. I happen to believe that we all come from somewhere, and that place explains who we are and who we want to become. There's a reason behind all the decisions I've made, and the stories I relate here, I think, reveal it.

THE CONCEPT

*Like socialism and capitalism, We and Me look like they're
standing at opposite ends of the line. But something
amazing happens when Me flips for We:
you can't tell one from the other.*

That's Weology.

Je ne suis pas un avocat.

In 1928 there was a painter named René Magritte who decided, at the age of 30, that he was going to paint a smoker's pipe. And so he did. The image shows the pipe in profile, a brown body with a black stem against a subtly shaded beige background. Beneath the pipe is written *Ceci n'est pas une pipe.* "This is not a pipe."

As any art aficionado will tell you (Google included), Magritte's work challenges your *perceived perceptions* of reality. That was his goal, to question what he saw. This canvas in particular—titled *La Trahison des images* (The Treachery of Images)—expresses Magritte's core idea. He said so himself: "The famous pipe! I have heard so many criticisms. Nonetheless, can someone fill my pipe with tobacco? No, in fact nobody can because it is just a representation. If I had titled my painting *This Is a Pipe*, I would be the liar."

So simple. The key to Magritte's painting is the lesson it aims to teach: that reality takes many forms and is shaped by trust (which comes once a person has tested a concept). It is a story reduced to its simplest, more objective form: the basic truth from a simple proof. The irony is that many people know about Magritte's famous pipe, but few can explain its meaning. Which makes it a paradox. Nonetheless, applied to a business, or any enterprise really, Magritte's way of thinking will come in handy.

Reality draws breath from truth, from proof. When I say *Je ne suis pas un avocat*, I'm telling you that I am not a lawyer. Yet if you look at the facts, at my CV, you'll find that I am a lawyer, with a law degree and membership in the bar and all that lovely stuff. In fact, with a bit of digging you'll find that I've worked in a law firm and that my first successes at ING were directly related to my legal expertise. Indeed, the lawyer in me paved the way, but maybe it was just the tip of the spear.

The way I look at it, my lawyer's training helped me and makes up a key part of my "package," but I feel that I did so much more than what a lawyer typically does. The understanding of law is just a set of tools that helps get a lot of jobs done.

And then, as mentioned, there's the basic truth. My legal knowledge is just a set of tools. Any other set of tools, like journalism or farming, could also be applied. The key is creativity. Creativity is the skill that lets me apply my legal tools in the first place.

No, I am not a lawyer.

Alterius non sit qui suus esse potest

The enemy of ambiguity is clarity. Be clear whenever you can.
—@PeterAceto, November 26, 2013, Tweet

I'm open to all kinds of learning, but in law school I refused to use Latin. No mens rea. No mea culpa. I never retained most of the terms despite being a "certified" lawyer because I refused to put them in my brain in the first place.

I wondered: Why does the legal profession, so full of intelligent people, use Latin? Even the Church stopped using Latin because it wanted the people to understand its messages. The Church wanted to be part of common vernacular because it would help it reach its ends: to connect with people. The Church did it, so why can't lawyers?

I don't know when I finally put the pieces together, but the answer is the exact *opposite* of why the Church moved away from Latin. The legal world wants to bedazzle people, to blind them with brilliance. It's how lawyers can keep charging high hourly fees: by following a cryptic code (having learned that code by heart at enormous expense). It's not just lawyers: it is any group of people who have created a special vocabulary they don't want ordinary people to understand. It's control. Control for accountants, engineers, doctors and, yes, bankers.

Yet, when I use the word *transparency* to describe the same thing—control—to those groups, they interpret it as a loss of control.

Transparency, to them, is inviting others to see what they shouldn't see: your mistakes, how you made a decision. Which is actually what makes transparency good—it keeps you on your toes. Everything is out in the open, the whole process. It's an open-source business methodology.

We use that transparency as its own means of control. I'll tell you exactly how. If you truly are transparent, if you truly treat your people this way, if you truly make decisions that balance what's in the best interests of your business and your customers, and in addition if your competitors don't and can't replicate it, then transparency can be a sword. You become stronger collectively by showing your vulnerability.

Not just any business can adopt this model. Because if you're truly transparent people will find things that you haven't seen; they will find the mistakes. Empowering clients makes us better service providers and gives them more incentive. (But only if you are willing and able to adapt when your transparency surprises you.) A good example straight out of the meeting rooms at Tangerine was our Non-Sufficient Funds (NSF) fees policy and one client's phone call.

This is how it worked. If, say, your mortgage payment bounced, the NSF fee was $35. But if you did the exact same thing when you were *depositing money* into your savings account (from another bank, say), it was $25—which doesn't make any sense because managing the NSF process takes the same amount of time whatever account is involved. This was an oversight on our part. Eventually, a customer noticed and called us out on it, and we realized we were the ones making the mistake. So we changed: our NSF fee became $25 across the board. We just admitted the mistake and moved on.

The issue merits defending. And by defend I mean helping people understand your perspective. Which leads to the question: Why is it that some banks charge $50 or even $60 for an NSF penalty? I'll never say that all fees are bad—the bank has to make money too. Our customers understand that we are a business, and if we don't make money we don't get to keep doing what we're doing, and they don't get the value they get. I believe that many of our competitors charge those fees precisely because they can, and they charge the most they possibly can. They make money from customers who either don't understand the fees they pay or don't care. That's what phone companies and Internet providers often do too. They make a lot of money from customers who don't know better or don't care to read every line of the small print. I can only imagine what the return is on consumer ignorance.

We do charge an NSF fee however. We do this because when you send us a cheque without sufficient funds in the account, there's a list of things that we need to do that involve people and time. For that, we deserve to make a fair margin in exchange for the service we provide. I have no trouble saying to a customer, "This is work that you caused, which is why you have to pay for it." I think that's reasonable, and what I'm aiming for in my relationship with customers is to be given the benefit of the doubt. No customer is happy to learn that he or she has to pay fees for a mistake, but I expect they'll respect and understand why it happens.

So why do lawyers use Latin? It must be to justify charging someone $600 an hour. My view is people will still pay $600 for a good lawyer—for other reasons. They don't have to make it so that no one understands what they are saying.

I didn't decide when I was a lawyer that I was going to become dedicated to transparency; I gained this outlook over time. My feelings turned into clear images: direction, a place to go, a North Star, a vision.

WHAT do the words of Paracelsus, *Alterius non sit qui suus esse potest*, mean? "Let no man be another's who can be his own," or more simply, just be yourself.

Always take the last shot,
and remember Aristotle

The concept of working to benefit the collective, the We, was deeply ingrained in me from my earliest days at the bank. As part of the legal team, I needed to deeply understand the rules and laws of banking and to help the team figure out ways to simplify things for our potential clients.

As is often the case, the rules that regulate an industry do not keep up with how technology, consumer preferences and innovations are changing that industry. When we started in Canada, the rules made little sense from a consumer's perspective. If Jennifer wanted to move money from her bank account to her newly opened ING Direct savings account, she needed to go to her bank and instruct them to do it for her. Ask "them" to send her hard-earned savings to a competitor.

Obviously, sending our customers back to our competitors to have this awkward conversation would not set us up for success. "Good morning, I am here to ask you to please send $10,000 over to my ING account." Once the customer's decision to switch was made, it needed to happen right then. Otherwise, the competitor bank could decide to charge fees or penalties; it could say *No, don't do this*, or it could try to convince the customer to stay, somehow. Maybe the bank would even take this opportunity to treat its customer better than it had chosen to before. Although this might serve the interests of the established banks, it was not the making of a successful, disruptive business model that benefited Canadians.

In other words, the big banks always had the last shot, and we knew that wasn't going to work for us. After all, it doesn't work this way in any other industry. Why should consumers be forced to face the company they want to leave? It's awkward, it can be unpleasant, and it can be avoided. When you decide to stop eating at a restaurant because the food or the service isn't any good, do the rules force you to go to that restaurant and tell them how you feel before you can eat elsewhere? Obviously not.

The success of the business would depend on our customers' ability to give us instructions to withdraw money from their accounts at their other bank without giving the existing institution another chance to finally do things right, or worse, to impose punitive fees to trap customers. In our minds, if they hadn't done you right by that point, why should they get another chance?

An institution that wanted to move money through the Canadian banking system needed to be a member of the Canadian Payments Association (CPA), which is mostly controlled by the large, established banks. The CPA created the rules that govern the movement of money through the system. The CPA is important and fundamental to a safe and secure financial system, but the rules were never designed to be friendly or open to new ideas, new business models or new competitors. Specifically, there was no provision to allow a depositor to give an institution clear instructions to pull their money out of one account in one bank and transfer those funds into a new account with another bank.

Changing these rules was not in the best interest of the established banks. But it sure would be good for us, and especially for our customers, so we focused on this issue to start. As the bank's legal counsel I saw myself as a key part of our strategy. My mission was to figure out new ways of navigating the existing rules and to find innovative legal solutions to help our business be successful. It was an exciting time and an exciting role. The goal was to always honour the spirit of the rules, which ensure a safe and sound banking system, while working through the letter of the laws that were designed primarily for traditional face-to-face banking.

In my lawyer's mind, there's the spirit of the rule, and then there's the letter of the rule. The spirit of the rule was this: the regulators didn't want you to withdraw money directly out of your current bank account unless your other bank knew it was you, and unless they knew it was your account and unless they could do it in a safe way. So the issue was with the identification of the account holder and of the accounts, to ensure no errors could be made. Everything had to be just right, always.

Also because of the rules in Canada, we did our payment clearing through one of our major competitors, which sounds odd—and it is. We began negotiations with our "direct clearer." It was our way of accessing the payment system. Our direct clearer insisted on putting limits on the amounts that could be transferred to a new account with us, and it brought up a whole variety of restrictions and conditions. We needed to be persistent.

Luckily, public opinion was on our side.

At the time there was political discussion about the lack of competition in the banking industry in Canada. There were no successful competitors that had reached any significant size. We knew we could make this money transfer a political issue, if needed.

After months of discussion and negotiation, we were able to get a new rule added to the Canadian Payments Association that allowed us to facilitate transactions the way we wanted while also codifying safe and sound practices around making these transactions. The regulation was called Rule A6 and it never looked very sexy to anyone but me. It was created to allow a customer to instruct a bank to pull money directly from another bank. It sounded so simple: I authorize ING Direct to pull $2,875 out of my "blue bank" chequing account and to put it into my ING Direct savings account.

When I look back at the pile of work required to start a bank, I realize how big this issue was for the company's success and for the millions of Canadians who have been paid billions in additional interest. We were trying to operate in a less competitive marketplace. We were trying hard to enter a marketplace with few true challengers. We wanted to create more choice, something different than Canadians had seen before.

I think all sides have won in the end. In the years since ING Direct Canada launched in 1997 we've paid over $6 billion in interest alone. This would have never happened without that rule change. We all would have missed that opportunity. Today there's a banking product category called "high-yield savings." It didn't exist two decades ago. Canadians are getting paid more than they ever have for their great savings habits. Not just our own clients; this change helped millions of Canadians earn billions of dollars regardless of where they bank. Today all of our competitors have high-yield savings accounts—everybody wins. And all we did, really, was eliminate a phone call. One single phone call.

What does Aristotle have to do with all of this? Well, he waxed poetic when he suggested that people are free to do whatever they want to do as long as their freedom doesn't hinder someone else's freedom. That was our thinking. At the end of the game, you want to have the ball so you can take the last shot. We'd rather be in control than hope for the other team to miss.

Screw the status quo

Whenever you find yourself on the side of the majority, it is time to pause and reflect. —Mark Twain

One of the world's best creative marketing companies was founded in Montreal and is called Sid Lee. One of the things I love about Sid Lee is the T-shirts and posters they print for employees. The font may change, but the message remains the same: "Screw the status quo."

For Sid Lee, this is more than just a T-shirt, and it's more than just a state of mind for how the company runs its business. It's a statement about the kind of clients they want to work with. They want challengers, people who want to change, to grow, to evolve into the number one position. They want to work with people willing to take risks despite the obvious costs. After all, who wants to work for *"Just give me the same old thing?"*

I like the Sid Lee thinking. So, too, have Cirque du Soleil, Adidas, Facebook and many other great global brands. What Sid Lee says makes sense to me, the challenger mindset. It's a good reflection of the way Tangerine operates. When we won the fight on Rule A6, it was because we persevered and didn't compromise. Perseverance in this case meant fighting for what was right—an easy call.

It was imperative that we have a direct relationship with our customers. Our business model depended on it. If we were going to change the game, we needed that direct link. We finally solved the problem from all the perspectives—interpretation of the law to payment transfer details and everything in between—because they're all connected.

We needed to challenge the banking status quo because, well, nobody else had in decades! The established banks didn't need to change because, in many ways, they were an oligopoly. Why change?

When you take a look at the banking system and the established banks, you find a collection of century-old companies with deeply rooted cultures. Although they are now more focused on clients, it was certainly less the case in the past. When a competitor with the means to change the game and how it's played entered the game, it was seen as a threat. The status quo is good for the established players. The speed with which the rules and regulations evolve and the way that new entrants get access to the system can really slow down a competitor or inhibit its success.

For us the idea was clear: have a simple, single differentiating goal. For the first time, we created an opportunity for the customer to choose without outside influence. Some might wonder why we felt we had to buck what many called a sound, working system. Well, what's your definition of *working*? It is true that we've had no banking failures in the history of our country, whereas the Americans have had seven or eight. I get it, Canadians need a safe and sound system, but does that mean it can't or couldn't ever evolve? No.

Safety at what price? Who paid for the cost of safety? Consumers did, primarily through one of the most expensive banking and investments system in the developed world. Low rates on deposits. High rates on loans and fees. The most expensive mutual fund fees in the developed world. Surely there was room for innovation and competition while maintaining a safe and productive system?

We are challengers. This has been one of our defining corporate values. We challenge the status quo. We challenge the way that

Canadians think about banking, the way regulators think about banking, the way Tangerine and its employees think about banking. It's embedded in our culture so we're trying to do new things, always. And always with the idea of helping Canadians live better lives.

We may not print cool T-shirts that tell people to "Screw the status quo," but I have to admit, that slogan is a great way to clarify things for everybody involved—you and your clients. Perhaps that's why *Forbes* magazine has referred to Sid Lee as one of the world's five best creative companies.

Clean the toilet

*Getting a grasp on the true reality of your business without any filters is
a huge benefit to any leader, particularly a CEO.*
—@PeterAceto, November 12, 2013, Tweet

My family and I are huge fans of the international phenomenon
we know today as Cirque du Soleil. We are amazed and daz-
zled with each show and wonder how they can continue to innovate
and surprise their audiences time and again. Guy Laliberté is the man
behind Cirque du Soleil, the most famous circus ever, an international
phenomenon that constantly reinvents itself. But he first performed
on the streets in Europe and in Quebec. He started as a folk musi-
cian, learning the harmonica and accordion, and on his overseas trav-
els busking across Europe, he picked up the art of fire-breathing and
expanded his street routine. Later, when he tried his hand at a "real
job"—working in a hydro plant in Quebec—he lost it after a labour
strike. This was when he joined a troupe of acrobats who specialized
in stilt walking.

In school, Laliberté had garnered experience at putting on events,
which helped him organize a large summer fair involving his troupe.
One show led to another. After a couple of years Laliberté got a big
break in 1984, winning the right to put on a huge celebratory event
in honour of Jacques Cartier's discovery of Canada. This gave rise to
the Cirque du Soleil—which was originally conceived as a one-time

thing until the provincial government provided a grant to turn it into a touring event.

Over the course of 25 years, Laliberté turned his circus into a multibillion-dollar company, developed the biggest theatre production group in history, and created work for thousands of circus artists and artisans across the globe. What genius.

I appreciate stories like these because they demonstrate how difficult it is to have success in any field. Laliberté went through the ranks even before there were ranks. He proved that genius walks next to relentlessness. He knew how to do every single job in the circus because he had done each one himself. Success does not just fall in your lap, it is usually well earned, deserved and fought for.

A leader has to know first-hand how the various aspects of the business work, or at least the fundamentals. There is no better way to learn than by being involved in the day-to-day of those areas. You can set proper expectations, set realistic goals and troubleshoot from experience gained, instead of having to delegate everything.

You need to prepare your career path by working in every department possible, raising your hand for all the opportunities that come near you, working honestly and giving everything to it. That's what I did. Raise your hand and fill your bucket with as many experiences as you can! Be greedy for experiences.

A friend of mine told me a similar story—but with different results. When he was still a teenager he worked at a famous Ottawa institution, Ritchie's Sports shop. It was the place to buy sports jerseys, caps and sneakers. During one shift when the store was quiet, my friend found the store manager washing the toilet. There was the boss, on his hands and knees, scrubbing away. So my friend asked him: "Why don't you let me do that job? You're the boss." To which the boss answered: "You'll get your chance to clean the toilet, but it's important that I know how it feels and what it takes. No job is too big or small for anyone." In addition to giving the manager an understanding of all work-related operations, working all jobs in the company earned respect from a teenaged staff member.

So just clean the toilet and it's another win-win.

The only shortcut is hard work

While leaders may lead others, they decisively lead themselves first.
—@PeterAceto, November 12, 2013, Tweet

I don't think it was any one thing I said that convinced our board to pick me as the new CEO of the bank in 2008. If you had asked them, they'd probably admit they were taking a risk. The company had taken similar risks in the past, and that had worked in my favour because embracing risk, finding new solutions to old problems and achieving success throughout was certainly part of my track record.

The most fortunate thing I had going for me was a wealth of *cross-functional* experience. I wasn't an expert in marketing or branding, but I'd spent two years working in those departments. I had not wanted to run the Risk Management division at first, either, but when asked I had said yes (of course). I felt confident in my appreciation of key departments and their operation, and that's crucial in decision making. There has to be a greater vision at work behind a leader's decisions, an ethos, and mine was constantly to get better. It still is.

As with everything worth fighting for, in business there are no shortcuts, no ready-made solutions. A lot of books or programs claim to have the secret, the magic bullet of sorts, but ask 50 leaders and I'll bet you'll get a host of different answers.

To get the CEO job, a small group of people have to decide

they're willing to give you absolute accountability for an entire business. The decision also depends, of course, on the business's needs at that given time. Everyone wants a failsafe formula, but in the real world it simply doesn't work that way, like get-rich-quick schemes that never get you rich quick.

If I were on a company board interviewing someone for the CEO job, my first concern would be around trust: I'm entrusting a multibillion-dollar business to this person, 1,000 employees, 2 million customers and a great reputation. I would want someone I can trust and believe in, someone who will be a good steward to rally the entire company. Someone who can execute the existing strategy, or who will create and implement the next one.

Not everybody can be a CEO. There are so many moving parts involved, some things you can control and some things that are out of your control. Everything has to converge at the right time, the person, the moment, everything that happened before and will happen later. I've met, read about or studied all kinds of CEOs, but I can't say there's one common thread that connects all of them. It may be something like ambition, but there are a great number of ambitious people who make awful CEOs.

So my idea is simple: hard work opens doors.

Make your luck

Some people have more luck than others. It's a good strategy to follow the luck. —@PeterAceto, January 9, 2014, Tweet

The most important people in your life often are the ones who don't believe in you. The ones who tell you No.

People generally tend to think that successful people are lucky. Fine. The most important thing about luck, though, is accepting it. You can only take opportunity if you're prepared for it. I was the guy who always put his hand up whenever there was an opportunity. *Always.* I truly believe I can succeed at any challenge. If you need someone to do something, I'm your man!

Why? Because of all the times I've been told No. Being told No makes a person hungrier. I don't like being told No, so I've decided to restrict my own use of the word. Saying Yes put me in some tough positions, and I learned from those experiences. I thirsted for them. When I was the head of legal at the bank, for example, I would know when someone was about to be asked to leave the company. I drafted all of the documents related to employee dismissals. So, as masochistic as it may sound, I would often ask to be in the room when "it" happened. Not to protect anybody, but because I was hoping, as I moved along in my career, that I would one day get to manage people. Until then, I wanted to keep learning and experiencing, and to see how leaders handled different situations, both good and bad. I wanted to be in the room, to watch and learn.

When ING needed a CEO to run their banking business in Italy, I put my hand up. My wife and I didn't really want to go, but I still put my hand up. I finished second, thank goodness, to a top-notch German guy with five more years of experience. Going through that process, though, was a great experience for me. I learned that sometimes luck is *not* getting what you think you want. I discovered that luck also grows from a negative outcome, whether you're the one who said No or someone else did it for you.

This topic reminds me of the most defining story of my career. One Saturday morning, back when I was a disillusioned young lawyer, my father needed to take his car to the mechanic. I went with him, and that was the day my life changed. While waiting and having a cup of coffee, we struck up a conversation with a man next to us who was also killing time. He seemed excited and willing to share his vision with any passerby. He was planning to start a new bank. A bank that would be different from anything the world had seen. It would treat customers in a way they had never been treated before. It would have better rates and no fees. It would use technology to wow people every day. It would be able to make a credit decision on a loan so fast that it would have to delay telling customers so that they believed the bank had properly weighed its decision to lend. It would be a bank with no fine print, no hidden rules, no bait and switch. It would be a bank that would change banking forever. This man's name was Arkadi Kuhlmann.

A chance meeting in a garage turned out to be the beginning of my relationship with my most influential mentor, the man who created ING Direct, the man who, for me, opened the door to another world. As you can imagine, I was incredibly moved by my chance meeting with Arkadi. All weekend, I could not stop thinking about his vision. I felt like an insect being drawn toward a flame—I was compelled to find him. After some digging I was able to get his phone number, and I called him on the following Sunday evening. I told him that I was excited about the story he'd told and that I'd really like to hear more if he could make the time for me. We met several days later and I offered my services. I told him I was a lawyer but would be willing to do anything to be a part of his vision and to help him make it real. I'd answer the phone, sweep the floor, but please give me a chance to help. After a few more meetings/interviews I was "the lawyer" for ING Bank of Canada. Actually it wasn't even a bank yet. That was to come later. Holy @#%! I was going to help start a bank!

Today, I shiver at the thought of *not* meeting Arkadi. If my father had chosen a different time, or a different day, or if I had been too lazy to go, too distracted, I would have become a completely different person. I would now live in a different world. My father and I could have thought: *Who is this man who keeps talking to us?* We might have zigged left instead of zagging right and sat down next to a plant and not the person who changed my life—and ultimately the lives of many who took the same journey.

Was this luck? Yes, the circumstance was lucky. But it's only lucky when I look back at it because if I hadn't acted on the opportunity, none of this would have happened. When luck presents itself, even if you're not sure it's the real thing, you have to attack the opportunity. You can't sit by and wait for it.

Arkadi will come up regularly throughout this book, because I remember so many lessons I learned while working closely with him. I'd been around enough people to know I didn't fit in the world of No and negativity. Arkadi had a way of sharing his vision that was enthralling. And what's more, he liked people who had scars, because he thought it put a chip on their shoulders, gave them something to prove. He gave me a shot at working in a bank even though I had no experience. He'd seen something in me, something I hadn't even seen. In other words, he said Yes to me, and so I said Yes to him.

Arkadi's preference for people with something to prove reminds me of the football player Tom Brady and his path to success. Brady is, arguably, the greatest quarterback in the history of American football. He has won the MVP trophy twice and the Super Bowl, and he owns a slew of records. But when we look at his career today, we tend to forget that Brady was the 199th pick in the 2000 draft. Being picked 199th in the NFL draft is equivalent to being the last kid picked for a game of dodge ball. The message is clear: *You kind of stink.* Six other quarterbacks were picked before Brady.

In his rookie season, he was the fourth-string QB for the New England Patriots. The first time he met the owner of the Patriots, Brady looked his new boss in the eye and told him that picking him was the smartest thing he'd ever done. What happened? In Brady's second season, the team's starting quarterback was injured in the fourth quarter of the team's second game. Brady stepped in and has been the Patriots' starter ever since. (There's a video on YouTube titled "The Brady 6," and it recounts the story of Brady and the six QBs who were picked before him and what happened to their careers—it's great content and worth watching.)

Many believe that Brady is lucky because he is, but what they discount is the way he has always been ready to make room for luck in his life. He was prepared, physically and mentally. And he always has something to prove, that chip on his shoulder.

There's been luck in my personal success. There was luck in meeting Arkadi that day. And there's been luck in the success of our business. But we, my team and I, did not just lie on the couch when stuff happened: when those doors of opportunity that we hadn't known about opened just a sliver, we moved with energy and decisiveness, determined to kick them open. From a timing perspective, being in the right place at the right time, luck plays a role in success.

In the simple, immortal words of Ernest Hemingway: "You make your own luck." That means recognizing opportunity and acting on it.

Don't stop at different, go for inimitable

They always say time changes things, but you actually have to change them yourself. —Andy Warhol

So if what Tangerine has been doing is so good, why don't other banks follow? The simplest answer is that so far they can't.

Scotiabank, which acquired ING Direct Canada in 2012, is 180 years old. Its management has a way of doing things. It has a culture that is significantly different from Tangerine's. It's got layers. It has shareholders in a different way than we ever will. It has branches nationwide. The culture, people, history and branches are many of the reasons why Scotiabank can't do what we do. The beauty of Scotiabank, and I discovered this from our earliest meetings after it purchased ING Direct, is that it understands how our differences can make us both better and stronger.

Maybe eventually the rest of the Big Five banks will be able to deliver similar service, and that's definitely part of their thinking, but they'll have to challenge the status quo in a rather revolutionary way. First of all, they've got that significant branch structure. Even though bankers in the U.S. and Europe are looking at decreasing their branch footprint, Canadian banks have actually been increasing theirs. Our operating model is incredibly different. In 2014, most of the larger banks had upwards of one thousand branches each, serving between seven and ten million customers in Canada. This is a typical ratio among the large Canadian banks. Tangerine has about 940 employees for almost 2 million customers. The big banks have lots of real estate and long-term leases, and lots of their customers would feel uncomfortable if those branches disappeared. Tangerine has never had any branches.

It would be difficult, maybe impossible, for one of the banks to do as we do and become almost entirely online with no physical presence. It would be transformational and have a significant short-term impact on the business. This transformation would require a very difficult risk-reward discussion. It would just cost too much in the short term.

Could the established banks do 25 percent of what we do? Or 50 percent? I believe they can. I think it's possible that a big bank in Canada could compete with Tangerine directly. It could open a separate subsidiary under a different name and put in a different management team. It could do everything that Tangerine does. But it would take too long to get the payoff that shareholders would feel comfortable with. It would experience cannibalization of its existing customer base. This would be very painful in the short term, and it would be difficult to stay the course.

Tangerine was built to foster and focus on developing long-term relationships with our customers. Everything goes into that relationship process, including profits. I think the Big Five would have trouble with the willpower and patience involved in this way of doing business.

What we sell is good for our customers and good for Tangerine at the same time. It's the way our business model works. We all win. And that's what makes us not just different but, in many ways, inimitable.

We made the established banks' weaknesses our source of power.

Keep the light on in your office

Without solitude no serious work is possible. —Pablo Picasso

A good friend of mine who worked in politics on Parliament Hill a number of years ago once told me how a chance meeting on a downtown Ottawa street changed his life drastically and forever.

In certain jobs, especially those that revolve around politics or Parliament Hill, cocktail parties are innumerable. Indeed, if you know enough people, you can get a dinner of cheese, cold cuts, veggies, chicken skewers and wine or beer every single day of the week in Ottawa. The problem is that, after a while, these cocktail parties become a hindrance, a nuisance, a bore where lobbyists and favour-seekers hang out to corner members of Parliament, VIPs or their staff.

My friend was walking up the Hill toward another lame reception when he ran into a consultant who had worked in the office of Joe Clark (former prime minister of Canada) during the good old days. "How are you?" the staffer asked.

"I'm headed to another lame reception," my friend sighed.

"Why are you going if it's going to be lame?"

"I don't have a choice."

"You don't feel like going?"

"I'd rather go straight home, but I promised some people I'd be there."

36

The staffer's eyebrows lifted in unison, and then he peered over both of my friend's shoulders, the left then the right, looking for the person holding the gun to his head. "Ah, I see. Well, I'm going to do you a favour. I learned a lesson in my early days of politics. People will pull you in all directions and everything is urgent and important and every event is key for re-election. But you and I both know that's not true. Right?"

"Right."

"So here's the lesson: don't do anything you don't want to do," he advised.

"That's it?"

"Yes, that's it. Follow that rule and you'll be 25 percent happier right off the bat. And if someone doesn't like it, tell them you're working. No one can argue with that, not on the Hill." The consultant smiled and strolled away.

Makes sense.

A couple of years later this same friend was working in the Prime Minister's Office, which meant two, sometimes three cocktail invitations every single day and constant lobbying to show his face. There was nary a moment to enjoy the canapés, between the lobbyists and the sycophants. And what did he do? He decided not to do anything he didn't feel like doing, which meant not going to most of those events. It created a different kind of win-win: he won when he did attend because people noticed his presence, and he won by not going because he had planted the seeds of his story, which helped build his reputation. The story is what made it all come together. He'd say: "I can't come to the event tonight, too much work to do. But if you drive by the Langevin Block on Parliament Hill, you'll see the light on in the third office from the main door. Wave hi as you drive to the party, and drink one for me."

The business equivalent to the political cocktail circuit is the infamous rubber chicken dinner. Truth is, the food is usually pretty good (and often not chicken!), but you know what I mean. There are better ways of spending Friday nights, and money too. For a while I started bringing colleagues from the call centre or operations associates, to give them a feel for how these gatherings work and maybe provide some inspiration and/or motivation. What's more, it was a way to reject the Establishment. Bringing several call centre associates to a business awards dinner was absolutely novel and in many ways odd.

And there it is: don't do anything you don't feel like doing, and keep the light on in your office at night so people will *know* you chose duty over party.

Define happiness

Create your future from your future, not your past. —Werner Erhard

The most dreaded question anyone can ask me is "What are your long-term goals?" Because I don't know what my personal long-term goals are. I don't have a clue. I have a family and I want us to be together, to be happy and healthy. I'd also like to retire at some point. But who doesn't want these things?

When Scotiabank acquired ING Direct in 2012, my new boss asked me what I wanted to be doing in 10 years. I'm guessing that he wanted me to say, "I want to be right where you're sitting." The problem is that I didn't actually want his job.

If I were sitting down with a financial planner, and we were going to do a written plan, my goal would be to retire when I'm 55. Meaning I wouldn't have to work anymore if I didn't want to. That I'm free. That I can stay and survive in expensive Toronto and not have to relocate to small rural community. And that I'm able to send my kids to the university or college that they want to attend in order to pursue their passion.

I don't genuinely believe I'm going to stop working when I'm 55, but I certainly would like to be in the position where I could. But that's about all I know of the future, and none of it is too concrete. In fact, I love my work, the mental challenge, the complexity of leadership, the challenge of solving problems, the satisfaction of being on a team, so I'm not sure I'd ever want to leave these pleasures behind.

I love being in the banking business. I enjoy being on a team that achieves amazing things. I feel good being on a team where, if you lose, you're still a team and, if you win, it's because of the team. You see people surprise you, in terms of skills and abilities. You see people who start in the call centre as associates and become senior executives. Just watching and contributing to their growth and success is awesome.

The goal is always to show people that they can achieve great things, deliver great projects that they never thought possible. Breaking that thought pattern and being able to show people their creation, to let them see how their idea came to life, is powerful. It means something. It changes the way you look at your colleagues, your team. There are these moments, just like in the movies, when you catch the other person's eye and share a quiet moment, a slight nod that says it all.

I like that I can actually feel the business, that I can get on the phone, go on the Web site and say, *I think this process can be a lot easier*, and fix it. I can actually talk to customers. I don't want to spend my time at head office, managing office politics, looking at reports, being senior, being disconnected from the product, the people, our clients. I still do some of that, but I like the intimacy of being a part of a business.

I think the success of the business and my personal success are incredibly linked. My success in my family life is important to me too, and they're always pulling at each other, and more here means less there, and vice versa. But they are tightly knit.

I know that I don't need more than what I already have. It's always nice to have more than what you need because it means there are fewer things to want, but the effect wears off after a while. The second car feels good, but not as good as the first one. The second house may be bigger and more comfortable than the first one you owned, but it's still number two. But the experience of getting better at your job, of winning bigger battles, is as addictive as getting new things, but it delivers a bigger bang.

So just find a way to be happy in your work by knowing the difference between want and need.

Once you've climbed the mountain, don't dwell on the view

Success breeds complacency. Complacency breeds failure. Only the paranoid survive. —Semiconductor pioneer Andrew Grove

After Scotiabank bought ING Direct, I wanted to continue for 18 months in my role, so that was the deal I made with my new boss. I said, "I promise you I'll give you the best I've got for 18 months and then we'll talk again." We shook hands and shared a brief hug.

There were things that needed to be done and I wanted to lead that process—this included, of course, rebranding the bank and developing a strategy to drive the business forward. Luckily for me, he accepted my proposition.

I suppose I could have joined an executive rotation program that shuttles executives into various positions in various places. There would still be a day-to-day routine, but the priorities would shift from what I'd made them—from being at the centre of the buzzing hive to managing and handling top clients.

I thought about his proposal and discussed it with my wife. I could have decided *Yeah, I'll just be "on the program," do the work that needs to be done and cruise.* But the more I thought about it, the more I knew I couldn't live my life that way. Admittedly, part of me would have liked to hear "You've been here 17 years. Here's a big chunk of

42

money; now get out, you're fired." I could have spent the summer with my family. I could have done a lot of things. But deep down, that option wasn't for me.

One of my most critical needs, maybe the most critical one, is the need to continue to evolve and grow. It's the equivalent of climbing mountains. I like climbing mountains, and if there's not a new mountain to climb I get bored super-fast and will definitely be moving along. Repositioning the brand and the business was a huge challenge, so I had another mountain to climb, the toughest one I'd ever faced.

Scotiabank paid Dutch parent ING Groep $3.126 billion for ING Direct Canada (and none to me by the way, for all those people who wrote me emails calling me a sellout). The Street thinks they overpaid, but I believe otherwise. Over time, this deal will have been one of the greatest Scotiabank has done.

That's the thing about mountains: I'm pretty interested in climbing them and not very interested in looking at the view once I'm at the top. Many mountaineers will tell you they climb because of the journey, not the summit. Once they reach the summit, some climbers will bivouac, hydrate, take a short rest and then descend.

I love this business but if I were told, *Don't change anything you're doing for the next three or four years, status quo*, I wouldn't be getting what I need personally from my job. I'd have to find something else to do.

I know some successful types who are more special ops–style executives, in and out stealthily, ruthless when they have to be. I wouldn't say I'm exactly that way, although I love a crisis—that is to say, I perform well in crisis. I'm quite calm and good at dealing with such issues. They become stimulating.

When you are climbing the mountain, everything becomes sharper. You see things clearly, briefly—and then you find another mountain to climb.

Selective disclosure

Life can be so much more fun if you can rid yourself of the guilt that comes with always letting someone down.
—@PeterAceto, March 4, 2014, Tweet

A simple way to look at and analyze the workforce—specifically, people's level of happiness—is to conduct what is commonly called a climate check, but what I like to call the "umbrella test." It works in a few succinct steps, formulated as questions: (1) What climate do I experience in my job? (2) What's the climate for the people reporting to me? (3) What's the climate for the people who report to them?

I like how the tabulated result paints an immediate picture of the situation and pinpoints the likely source of the problem.

If the climate's really bad at the top, and it gets worse as you go down in the organizational structure, you know what's happening: management is making it worse, not better, as you go down. This is not a good situation to be in, to say the least. Essentially, it means the entire place is in some form of unhappy crisis, and it probably starts with you.

If the climate is rough at the top but then improves as you move down through the same structure, it means, obviously, that the people who report to you are somehow making the situation better—they're acting as the umbrella. They're shielding and deflecting the bad weather coming from up top. This is an improvement compared to the first example, and it also represents a form of hope, something to build on. It means you've got a solid core, which is fantastic, and that you're the one who needs to change.

What I've learned over the years is that my job is to try to shelter those below me from the inclement weather up at the top. But playing the part of umbrella is not always enviable. Sometimes, the person holding the umbrella is stuck in a position that compels him or her to hold back on the truth, "white-lying" to colleagues.

Rightly or wrongly, if people knew everything going on all the time in any business, nothing would ever get done. People would become overly worried about their jobs and everything that implies about losing your home, financial health, car payments . . . life! No, worry doesn't help the organization or the individual, so the key is to get rid of it. Hence the umbrella. It's not always fun to be the one holding the thing, but that comes with responsibility and is part of decision making. At some point, as the leader, your job is to make a decision. To act because the situation demands it. To know that the whole truth, at this stage, won't get any more "whole."

I'm sure there are many leaders who remember the financial crisis that began in 2008. I certainly do; those were still my early days as CEO, and ING Direct was not immune to the downturn. I was part of a global management group that discussed just how bad things were every day. Every single morning my alarm went off at 4:20 a.m. The bosses were in Holland, with colleagues joining from all over the world, and there I was in my pyjamas, alone in the office at home, holding a large cup of coffee and dialing in to the global management conference call that came every single day at 4:30 a.m. sharp.

The simple way to describe our situation was that it *felt* like we were near the precipice, and that these were more than just tough economic times. That's what it felt like, anyway. The problem with that kind of doomsday information is that it doesn't help to keep people focused on the job at hand. And the only way out of a crisis is by relying on solid, focused employees performing at their best, performing as a team.

I knew we had to keep doing what we were already good at doing, so I made a decision. I decided to distil the information from that 4:30 call and decipher what was relevant to share and what wasn't, and with whom. I had a singular purpose: to keep my people focused on their own work, on their own lives. Limit the worry, limit the fear.

At some point, you will have to acknowledge the human condition. Some people do not deal well with any kind of change, so why create uncertainty? As a leader you have to accept human nature; it is not something that you can control, and this can be a hard lesson to learn.

Here's the way I see it. If an employee's function isn't directly connected to the object of worry, why let him in on the nasty secret? Like water off an umbrella, bad news tends to cascade. It turns into worry, which kills focus, which affects performance, which hurts business, which harms the numbers, which turns into more worry . . . Indeed, it becomes a self-fulfilling prophecy.

Each person within the team has a role and the information necessary for delivering results for that specific role. At some point every employee will be informed of what's transpired or what's going on, but in a crisis situation we need to perform. The performance is all about "the We," while emotion is usually only about "the Me."

This nice expression sums it all up: "Worry is like a rocking chair. It keeps you busy, but it doesn't get you anywhere."

And sometimes you have to tell colleagues little white lies for totally different reasons. In 2014 we rebranded and changed our name from ING Direct to Tangerine. This was 16 months after our sale to Scotiabank. As part of the process I was supposed to meet the then CEO of Scotiabank to get final approvals for our new name—Tangerine. This was so important to me, to the team.

And I missed the meeting!

We'd been through the entire process, decided on the new name, and I'd already gotten my boss aligned with our thinking. I had to go see the incoming CEO at Scotiabank and represent a large team that had worked hard for 12 months during the transition, and I had to do it alone. I had left nothing to chance, over-prepared meticulously the night before. The meeting was at 1 o'clock in the afternoon. I could have sat at Starbucks from 8 o'clock in the morning on, but that would've been a bit much. And so I left the office in the northern part of Toronto and drove my own car (with plenty of buffer time before the meeting). But there was an accident on the Don Valley Parkway, and I was stuck in it. I couldn't get off. I couldn't move forward. I couldn't move back. Sitting there, powerless, it dawned on me: this is the professional equivalent of "The dog ate my homework."

A half-hour before the meeting was going to start, I called my boss and told him the situation. I'd only known him for a few months. I told him that I was stuck in traffic—the first such call I've ever had to make. Disappointed, he told me not to worry, he would handle everything. The fib? When I called my team they asked me how the meeting went, and I said, "It went well, we got what we needed, we got the green light"—an abridged version of the truth. But why? How could I steal their victory from them? This was not about me and what I did. It was about the outcome and a great victory for the team.

I was deeply embarrassed and wholly disappointed that I'd let down people who had given me their full trust, all the women and men who were working on this pivotal project. When we discussed it, my boss just said not to worry. The groundwork had been laid over time and well in advance. This meeting was not going to be controversial. However, I should have been there. It was important to me that he know that I cared an awful lot about it.

Why lie to my colleagues? Yes, it made me feel better, and sometimes that's okay. But they deserved to feel the elation they had earned and I couldn't have muffled that. Sometimes you don't have to torture yourself more than you deserve, even if the dog eats your homework or if you forget the lending rates. These things don't change the quality of your character. They just make you human . . . and a little white-lie teller.

Prepare your improvisation

Leadership is about having the courage to move the needle
for an entire organization despite your fears.
—@PeterAceto, November 12, 2013, Tweet

The first thing I did was iron my shirt and give the suit a quick pressing. Then I chose the tie I was going to wear, the shoes, the socks and even the underwear. Once these were ready I put the shirt in a bag, added a replacement blazer and took them to the car to hang overnight.

I had feelings of childlike excitement and apprehension the night before we made our public announcement of the name change of our bank to Tangerine, and so I over-prepared, as per usual. The goal was to minimize the risk that I was not going to be able to find, well, anything. Socks, tie, the works. I could basically be in a coma come morning and still get out on time—and not forget a thing.

Preparation: it just makes me feel better. I spot every bit of potential risk and try to mitigate it. What I'm really doing is removing extraneous details from my mind so I can focus on the goal at hand. Normally, once I get home, I ask the kids about school and we try to eat together. My daughter likes to use the computer, and the boys like to play mini-sticks floor hockey, so I play with them. And then I clean the kitchen with my wife because she often makes dinner.

But the night before we would tell the world what our new name would be, I was more withdrawn than usual. I needed to be a little more "inside" myself. That's how stress manifests itself, when I feel apprehensive, or nervous, or anxious. And my way of dealing with stress is over-preparation. So I just prepare and iron and press and fold and prepare.

It was a fairly complicated day we had organized, like a play with lots of transitions. Tangerine likes to make a big fuss when we do something new. When we launched the no-fee chequing account, for example, we organized a major press and public event at the Eaton Centre in downtown Toronto. Thank goodness people came. That's just our way of doing things. For the Scotiabank announcement there were pre-launch media interviews in the morning. There was a run-through of logistics for the day. Then the show at the Toronto Arts Centre and the content I had to deliver, which was basically a series of speeches.

I don't need much in the way of speaking notes because most of what I do comes from the heart, but I usually have some. There is so much information that needs to be delivered, in a certain order and on a timely basis—you can't just go on and on and on. That's why I write some stuff down. In preparation, I just keep reading the material over and over again. I have to be comfortable enough with the content so I can look at the audience. You can't just read to people, because they have to get a sense that you actually believe in your message. Making eye contact with the audience, connecting with people, makes speeches better.

If I don't use notes at all, people get a real sense of innate genuine passion and know I really believe the message.

And so for the Tangerine launch, I was the guy who had to deliver most of everything. It wasn't just to my employees. There were media, shareholders, tons of customers, the country! We sensed the world was watching. It was by far the biggest commitment in the most public way of anything I've ever done.

When I looked at the whole speech, soup to nuts, it was talking about our brand, our history, what we do, what we care about. It was all leading up to one moment: everyone just really wanted to hear what the new name was. The intricate program, which other people put together, led to that moment. There was a magician, live music, guest speakers, 14,000 people watching online, and I had to step out of this big magician's box and reveal the name, alone. What a naked feeling! Standing there in the pitch dark, all I could think about was the sign I was to hold and whether or not it was right side up.

I would say it was an amazing moment, but it was too scary for that. There was so much anticipation, and most people did not know what the outcome was going to be. This could be the biggest failure of my life or a triumphant victory for the team. The whole worry was about that moment, what people would think when they saw that name, *Tangerine*. Even the name was a huge risk. It was like climbing Everest from the other side. I had been able to hire and work with arguably some of the best marketing and branding experts in the world. It was still a climb, and still uncharted, but I knew Tangerine was the right name, the right brand for us.

Part of the tension derived from this event being the first big thing we did with the new shareholder, Scotiabank, in the room. The tendency might have been to play it safe, but we didn't do that. The way we went about sharing it, with our event, was unheard of. The only way we could pull off such a natural-feeling event and give it such an improvised feel was to manufacture it ahead of time with over-preparation.

In other words, the best improvised speech you'll ever give is written well ahead of time, and ironed nicely too.

Define success your way

In life and work, are you following the recipe or are you creating a recipe for something new? —@PeterAceto, February 21, 2014, Tweet

In the early 2000s, I was still the kind of man who wanted my weekend planned a day and a half in advance. I sought out a world of organized living, of symmetry, in which everything had its place. Everything but a speck of dust.

How times change . . . A decade later, I no longer want any of that. The new me seeks out the unstructuredness of the weekend. Even with hockey practice for the kids and those types of things, I crave the chaotic potential of an active long weekend.

I've just become much less anal, less organized, less fastidious. My office at home is messy. I don't actually like that 100 percent of the time, but a part of me does, because it's different from who I have been in the past. It feels like a progression. I don't know why exactly this pleases me so. Is it an experiment, an attempt at trying new things? Do I need some disorder in my life? Does it affect my structure at work? Or does it point in the other direction, one that lets creativity find its place?

Under stress a person goes to his or her natural tendencies. Maybe preparedness and organization are my natural tendencies, but I enjoy seeing that I can be more complicated than that. I don't go out of my way to make my home office messy. Sometimes it gets a bit over the top and then I can't resist, and I spend a nice half-hour tidying up. A treat . . .

For my family it's not always helpful to be so conscientious about being prepared. For example, I really hate being late. But from time to time, my wife makes me late. I don't like it, and she knows that. I usually make a fuss over it. I fuss about the time we need to leave to make the time we need to arrive by, and so on. It's because I've built in buffers, and I'm always planning to arrive 20 minutes early, just in case. It really bothers me to think there's even a hint that I could be late for a commitment, but then we arrive on time and I've given my wife the gears and, yes, I feel a deep sense of shame . . . But it does mean a lot to me to be on time.

Hopefully someday I won't *need* to be so on time.

Changing the way people think about things, influencing them and seeing what comes out of it gives me great joy. It provides a sense of accomplishment that applies to both my personal and professional life. I've lived through and seen a lot of negativity and unhappiness, and all I want is positivity and happiness for me and those around me. Doesn't everyone?

From a professional perspective I am trying to help people be happier. I believe that if they are better informed, if they opt for a life of active awareness, if they can simplify their existence, they will be happier. Consequently, they'll continue to improve every facet of their lives. More control, less stress, and I can contribute in my own small way.

In the bigger scheme of things, I often wonder about my personal philosophies and how I apply them to business, or the other way around, taking things from business and applying them to my personal life. It's confusing on many levels because I change, too. I evolve and get better. Sharper. The sum of these things means that ideas and priorities change with me.

Professionally I really want to be successful, I really do want success. I'm just not always sure how to measure it. It's not a constantly increasing salary or constantly increasing level of power. I just want success. So if our business succeeds and I can be successful, that's one way to measure it. Taking my boss's job would be a form of success for sure, but I don't want that success and I don't want to do whatever it takes to have that type of success. Gunning for individual success at all costs leads to a loss of focus.

Developing better people and investing in developing a better quality of life for humans are my top priorities. If the people in the company grow, and if the people at Tangerine experience individual success, the company will succeed, and then I can look in the mirror and feel proud. Every customer who comes away after each interaction with a better understanding of their finances, with a better feeling about their future, with more control over their lives, is a measurable success.

What does it all mean? That the only person who can truly define what success is for you is you.

Screw 'em if they can't take a joke

Orange is the happiest colour. —Frank Sinatra

Envision a stage with a big screen behind it. On either side of the screen are giant banners proudly reading TANGERINE. We had just shared our new name with the world. I did not know that we had given the band we'd hired for the occasion a special request to curb the cursing, if possible, and deliver a PG show. Although I'm assuming we did not specify that this extended to screen projections . . .

Anyway, the band happened to be Grammy-winning Macklemore & Ryan Lewis. Why not? They'd bucked all the conventional ways; they'd managed their career and had successes without a label. Before they came on stage I had the privilege of introducing them to our audience. I said that there was a parallel between the band and the bank, and that, like us, they were true innovators. They had challenged the traditional.

They played a fantastic set, especially considering it was four in the afternoon in front of a sober crowd, and everybody danced. Their most popular song was titled "Thrift Shop" and it contained a few curse words. However, for our crowd they played the radio version, nice and clean. They also had a great visual show on multiple screens around the stage. These, however, did not get cleaned up. And at the moment of truth during their most popular song they sang (radio version), "This is really awesome!" but the large screens behind them said, "This is fucking awesome!" Suddenly Mark, one of my guys, asked me what he should do. He was worried about the Scotiabank people in the room, our customers and the analysts watching the Web cast. I looked at him and said, "Mark, you did everything right. The event is fantastic. What happened, happened, but you have to admit, this is fucking awesome! Great work, Mark. You and your team have done something fantastic. You should be proud."

The words on that screen, right next to our new name, actually fit quite nicely. We are trying to stand out from the competition. I thought it was absolutely priceless. The image was all over social media. And none of it came back to us in a negative way. Not a word! And even better, our employees were excited. There was a buzz in the room.

The Scotiabank team reacted exactly the same way. They proved they weren't micromanagers either, and people saw that, which made the event a powerful experience. A convincing one. In many ways a test of Tangerine's conviction.

I don't know how a typical bank would have organized a launch like that one, definitely not the way we had done it. That's why there's an understanding that we are different. Part of my job is to make clear how different we are from, well, the rest of them. So that every time any person interacts with us it feels, just, different. And good.

If we indeed are different, one of my jobs is to ensure people believe it. The only way to do that is to provide an experience that provokes emotions. People remember emotions. I really like what Confucius wrote about emotion: *Tell me and I will forget. Show me and I will remember. Involve me and I will understand.*

People who are involved are people who feel emotion. They become involved because they have felt the connection. And if that doesn't work, there is a lesser-known Confucian edict: *Screw 'em if they can't take a joke.*

Manufacture discontent

*If you want something you've never had, you must be willing to do
something you've never done.* —Thomas Jefferson

It seemed weird the way he put us together: Arkadi Kuhlmann hired
people who he liked to hang out with. People with dents and old
wounds who were driven by desire. People who'd had major career
setbacks and had overcome them. They'd faced adversity, scraped,
fought, coped and survived, and then risen.

It worked, too.

We weren't from prominent families, people who'd grown up with
four pairs of deck shoes for spring, the well-to-do Harvard types.
We were outcasts. There were about 20 of us in what Arkadi called
his posse. There was one particular guy on the team, we'll call him
Norman, who was unique even for an Arkadi-type misfit. He turned
out to be one of the smartest people I'd ever met, but I thought he
was quite a jerk. Norman was part of Arkadi's first posse and a key
pillar in the overall scheme. He and the boss had years of history
together.

I clearly remember our first meeting because it was quite unpleasant. Every year the management came together at the boss's cottage
for a few days' retreat for team bonding. I had just agreed to join the
U.S. team but hadn't moved to the U.S. yet. Because I was driving
my own vehicle to the retreat, Arkadi asked if I'd bring Norman. Of

course I agreed. I don't find it difficult to connect with people, not usually anyway. I want to like people. Unfortunately, I remember really not liking Norman from the get-go.

Ours wasn't a conversation among peers; it wasn't two people enjoying a ride on a country road. Instead Norman delivered a monologue interspersed with soliloquies. I was flabbergasted and thought, *Two hours in a car and you don't even try to connect with me?* It was no give, and all take. I later learned, of course, that sharing and exchanging ideas was not Norman's strong suit. He did not connect with me because I was still junior to him. It wasn't a good first impression for either of us. I wanted to establish fraternity while he was establishing seniority.

The obvious reality is that you don't have to like everybody at work. It's important and helpful, but it's not the top priority, and it's not even necessary. Although I did not like Norman, I also knew that this was my problem. I figured, based on reputation, that he was great at his job, so I decided to focus on that. On work. I said to myself, *Let's get the job done and forget the rest.*

Hierarchy was less than a word to us back then: the view was no different from the top than from the bottom. Anybody could talk to everybody about anything. We were on a mission to get things done and it felt like our workplace was a "doing" workshop. Each of us had our station and our goals.

The turning point for me came when I felt Norman attacked my integrity. I was accused of lying, of going over people's heads. It was deeply unsettling. The claim didn't make sense—we weren't supposed to be about ownership of projects; we were about getting results and moving forward as an organization. The meeting where these accusations were made—in front of several others—probably lasted five minutes, but it felt like an eternity. It was a different way of viewing Einstein's theory of relativity! Upset and mortified are the feelings that stood out. A fight with a respected senior guy was not good.

On top of this, my support system was non-existent. I was junior to Norman in every way. He had an extensive and far-reaching network inside the bank, he was revered all around, and it would have looked bad of me to complain about him to our CEO, Arkadi. I remember feeling cornered, not liking it, and not knowing how I'd succeed.

I didn't know what I was going to do, but then I took a good look in the mirror and something happened. I saw what everybody else already knew. If you had asked anybody I worked with to hang a word around my neck, 9 of 10 people would have chosen the word *nice*. Yuck, but bang-on, I'm afraid. The truth is that I really aim to be a nice guy—and that's often a problem for an ambitious person in the corporate world. As I moved along my career I wanted to keep growing, but promotion rarely happens if the only thing you are to people is nice. I wanted to continue to be successful, and I couldn't do it with *Oh, Peter, he's the nice guy*. The nice guy is dead meat.

The only solution was action. I didn't want to drop *nice* completely, but I didn't want the tag hanging around my neck forever. Thanks to Norman, I saw an opportunity to make a bold move that could really help the company and remove the "nice" branding from my forehead.

As I saw it, an initiative my team needed to accomplish had stalled, and I was convinced Norman was the roadblock. I may not always remember the lending rate—but I sure understand the overarching ethos driving our way of business. So I analyzed my problem from a different angle.

It made me uncomfortable to think Norman had dug in on the issue. He had credibility, smarts and history, and yet now there was a brick wall between us. My only realistic option was to attack the wall head on and try to blast through it. It would define me or defeat me. One thing was for sure: I wasn't going down without a plan.

First, I needed to battle Norman in front of my peers and prove my worth as an equal. Second, the battle had to be about the business and not the personalities. I sensed that a fight against Norman could be a win-win: the company would win and progress, and I would win and grow in stature and value.

But there was a problem: In seven years at the bank, no one had ever seen me get angry with anyone or anything. There was no bite, barely a bark. They'd never seen me upset because I didn't think you were ever supposed to show that side of yourself at the office. I thought a leader was all about emotions removed and energy focused on the task. Do; get it done.

It wouldn't be long before the perception that I was just another nice guy would kill my brand, which meant I couldn't push through with work initiatives that were crucial to the company's objectives.

I was going to trigger a fight with the smartest guy in the company, the master of numbers and facts and research, the walking encyclopedia of financial knowledge. So I plotted an ambush.

Plotting the fight

I had to do what I had to do (in the parlance of old times). It's a cliché, but that doesn't mean it's not true. And so, as artfully as I could, I chose a setting for the confrontation: our weekly leadership team meeting. The controversial business issue was already on the agenda.

My getting angry would take Norman out of his comfort zone because you can't fight emotional arguments with just numbers and statistics. Especially not when the debate takes place before a jury of peers. Even the most rational person will agree that words trump numbers, much the same way that rock crushes scissors.

With the setting decided, the key became preparation. My perception was extremely realistic (and sobering): This guy is wickedly smarter than me, and he can refute anything I say with an intelligent argument; he is favoured by all of my peers; he is an intellectual and can manipulate big words; his numbers jargon is top-notch. Heck, even the stupid things he says sound bright and cheery. He was not my favourite person, but he impressed me all the time. Which meant he could and would use words and numbers in a complex and compelling argument. I would stick to simple words and ideas.

I remember a friend telling me the story of the time Faulkner provoked Hemingway, and how Hemingway responded the only way Hemingway could respond, directly and with intent, one man to another and to nobody else, to the end: *"Poor Faulkner. Does he really think big emotions come from big words? He thinks I don't know the ten-dollar words. I know them all right. But there are older and simpler and better words, and those are the ones I use."*

Norman never spoke loudly. He was analytical but unpredictable. Some meetings he'd sit there and not utter a word, unless someone asked for his opinion. And then there were other meetings where he'd take over, as if he were a different person.

The more I thought about Norman, the better he was at everything. Efficient with words, he constructed amazing arguments built on logic and lots of numbers and statistics. He appeared to be the most prepared person in the room, all the time, on every issue. That's how people perceived him—the guy whose homework was always done. No one could be that accurate all the time. Whatever he said, people seldom disagreed. We couldn't. We daren't. He was nearly impossible to refute because you didn't have numbers ready to go, just like that, on a dime. He was a formidable adversary, which was why it was best to leave him be.

(Before you see me as a cold, calculating meany looking to ambush people, it must be said that I tried every possible alternative I could think of to solve the problem without confrontation. This showdown was the last resort.)

The fight

Emotion and passion were not Norman's strong suits, but they were mine.

I sat in the meeting as if it were a poker game as I waited for the issue to come up on the agenda. The whole time I kept thinking: *Show you deserve to be at that table, that you belong there, that you're good enough. You'll want to back down but don't. Keep fighting until someone stops you.*

When the moment arrived, Norman spoke first. I let him go right to the last period. And then, for the first time in my professional life, I leaned in. I put my elbows on the table. I looked Norman in the eyes, pointed, and spoke, calmly. "This is a mistake and you know it," I said.

I raised my index finger and then pointed again, like I was giving a beat. "We aren't stalling anymore"—point—"We need to move forward"—point—"We've wasted enough time." Point and exclamation point. Or something to that effect.

It was as if there were no others in that room. Just the two of us. We sat directly across from one another. None of our colleagues had ever seen or heard me act like this. They raised their eyebrows. Norman backed up just for a moment, stunned by the attack. There was too much emotion now to build an argument with another set of numbers. Being an intelligent man, he knew it. He threw a few jabs and hooks of his own, but none landed. None that I recall, anyway.

My argument was connected to our company's overarching goals and not to my personal benefit. The choice he offered was status quo, which in that room was a sin. It represented lack of agility, which meant lack of success. It went against the overall plan, the brand, the way of our business.

It was the right time to fight. If I'd picked someone smaller to fight, I would have been the bully. You need to surprise people, and even if you lose, it's not that big a deal. A defeat that leads to success.

The opposite of the infamous Pyrrhic victory (which is a win at such high cost that it amounts to defeat).

In many ways the fight was less about the issue and more about me stepping up at that table and standing up to the champion and winning. It was a huge step toward becoming an equal at that table—from junior to equal. In the words of comic strip character Andy Capp: "The problem with being tolerant is that people think you don't understand the problem." But that doesn't mean you can't win a fight. It just means you don't start them.

Pick fights nobody thinks you're going to win. But be prepared to discover a certain amount of ruthlessness in yourself. And, win or lose, it's often beneficial to be perceived as bold and scrappy, even if you aren't.

The aftermath

I don't enjoy recalling this episode, despite its importance in my life. A part of me regrets it ever had to take place. Not because I am soft, but because after that day I knew I had the ability to be hard. Who would enjoy the recollection of that? Yet my feelings changed in the aftermath of that key confrontation. I felt like I belonged at the table. And I started acting like it.

As I look back now and read my own words, I am conflicted. I have trouble seeing how standing up to Norman changed other people's perceptions of me. Nobody's outward behaviour toward me had changed, necessarily. I interacted well with people outside of the meeting context, in the day-to-day, and we were a great team. I can't discount, then, the possibility that the issue might have been me all along.

As I tweeted late in 2013: "Our thoughts and what we believe about ourselves can either cage or unlock our potential."

And so the real conclusion is this: the only person who needed proof that I belonged at that table was—me.

Don't poke the bruise

Debbie Muir, Canada's synchronized swimming coach at the 1992 Barcelona Olympics, has a good lesson on how she turned struggle into opportunity. It's outlined in a fantastic book she co-wrote with Olympic gold medallist Mark Tewksbury titled *The Great Traits of Champions.*

When preparing a routine for the 1992 Olympics, Muir found that most of the team's performance was, in a word, poor. Yet, during her video review with the team, Muir decided not to address any of the negatives. Not one. Instead, she found an absolutely perfect 20-second sequence from the training session. Rather than focus on fixing the other two minutes and 40 seconds, she focused on the 20 seconds of brilliance and built on them. She focused on stretching those 20 fantastic seconds into 40. Then into 60. And then into 120, and . . . you get the idea.

Those first 20 seconds became three minutes of gold in Barcelona.

I'm often surprised how there aren't more people who draw inspiration from our Olympic athletes who spend their lives dedicated to a single pursuit. They work years for a few tenths of a second, or an extra centimetre in the dirt. These years are spent mostly in anonymity, and then one day millions of people who haven't smelled chlorine in four years are watching the Olympic backstroke final—and they want their athlete to win. Years of preparation and focus go into one single fragile shot at victory. That's why building on the positives is key.

It's easy to fall into a pattern where you spend most of your time focused on what might have been, or what is not going well. Time should be spent on that too, but being consistently focused on the negative gets you bogged down: you either become a perfectionist—afraid of risk—or are broken spiritually. We need to spend more time focused on what is going right and build on it. Most professionals already know when they've stunk up the joint. So why poke the bruise?

The great Muhammad Ali was also an Olympic champion. And he's the one, the poet, who summed it up best: "The fight is won or lost far away from witnesses—behind the lines, in the gym, and out there on the road, long before I dance under those lights."

Know the force you're fighting against

You must know inside yourself the right path to take. It's often against the wisdom of the group. —@PeterAceto, October 11, 2013, Tweet

When I think of Muhammad Ali, it's easy to understand what he was fighting for: he wanted to be The Greatest. Before ever even winning a title belt, Ali told anyone within earshot: "I am the greatest!" And then he went out and proved it. How he did so is actually the simple part.

Every single day, even though he hated training, he worked toward his goal. He sparred, skipped rope and watched his diet. He changed his lifestyle and what he put in his body, abstaining from the sweet things he loved the most. He developed strategies for each fight, tactics that would allow him to be the greatest, and maintained this approach throughout his career, culminating with his rope-a-dope strategy against George Foreman in Zaire.

What I find most interesting about Ali is not what he was fighting for, even though it made him great. No, for me it's what Ali was fighting *against* that made him the greatest of all time, the only eternal champion. It's his battles against the establishment, against authority, against a system that put him in prison and prohibited him from fighting during what would have been his prime years as a professional athlete. It's his willingness to stand for unpopular ideas, his acceptance of rejection, his courtship of the target he carried on his back for years that changed the course of history.

Not just because he won. Because he endures.

My favourite example of Ali's leadership is a quote of his I first read on a T-shirt worn by a skateboarder a few years ago. On the front of the shirt was a picture of Ali taken from a 1968 *Esquire* cover, depicting him as the martyr Saint Sebastian, his torso pierced through with arrows. Created by the legendary George Lois, it's one of the enduring images of the decade—the ultimate expression of what Ali fought against. And on the back of the shirt is a quote: "Wars of nations are fought to change maps: but wars of poverty are fought to map change."

That is the consummate Ali. A man who stands alone in a ring but who delivers victory to legions of people who would otherwise never stand a chance. A Me who focuses on the We without any clear personal advantage just because it's the right thing to do for humankind. Ali's war against poverty was a battle against ignorance, fear and blind hatred.

What we're doing at Tangerine (in a very different context) feels somehow connected to Ali's mission. We too are fighting for something I believe is noble: for financial health and empowerment, and to help people live happier lives. But it's what we're fighting against that makes Tangerine even more interesting. It distinguishes our quest and gives us an edge over the competition.

One significant change that Tangerine has made that sharply differentiates us from bricks-and-mortar banks is our Tangerine Cafés. They were created for a very specific purpose but became so much more over time. Our vision for what they will be is also very exciting. When you walk into one of our Cafés (and I encourage you to do so) you will be able to see, feel, smell what Tangerine is and how different we are from what you are used to. Sit down on a comfy couch, log into our free Wi-Fi, grab a freshly squeezed orange juice or an organic drip coffee from sustainable micro farms in Haiti. Watch the digital boards sharing local community events in the area, our social media feed, the news and featured businesses in the community. Our hope is that you will ask about Tangerine, and our people will gladly share their passion with you and hope to inspire you to begin your journey of living a happy, healthy, financially empowered life. Our Cafés are a part of their local communities. They are a 3-D interactive manifestation of our brand. It feels good to be there, comfortable, simple, easy and, yes, fun.

If you want to become a customer we will show you how, by directing you to one of our tablets and our "Become a Client" paperless application. We'll be there helping, but you need to do it yourself. And, by the way, you could have done the same from the comfort of your own couch, any time of day or night—simple, easy, hassle free.

We won't do transactions for you. You won't find tellers, lineups, pens on ropes or pushy salespeople. And yet, people who become clients in our Cafés end up being more engaged, buy more products from us and refer more friends and family to Tangerine. We love our clients and we love our Cafés.

We are taking our Cafés to the next level. In our downtown Toronto Café we have exciting co-working space where entrepreneurs (nearly 100 of them) start their businesses up and run them. Being a part of this community has made many wonderful connections for us. We don't have any products that these businesses need, so selling to them is not our objective. We are one of the most client-focused banks in the world. We aim to redefine the client experience, and partnering in the future with innovative, entrepreneurial, client-focused people will create wonderful outcomes for everyone—for the We.

Tangerine is faced with overcoming more than a century of

people's expectations of traditional banking, combined with their fears of digital banking. So perhaps the best way to end this chapter is with a simple question: *Do you know what you're fighting against?* Because that's the real key to reaching goals.

THE MACHINE

*We (the collective) requires a structure that allows Me
(the individual) to shine. A machine that appreciates the way a
person thinks and feels, that is equipped with an operating system
that helps the collective, all because it was designed to change and
adapt to human nature. To the individual. To personal whims
and goals. Like a computer that feels its way forward.
An artificial structure that processes emotion.*

I am not a manager.

In 2008, just a few weeks before I returned to Canada from the U.S. as the newly minted CEO, I realized that, like it or not, I was about to become a manager.

As part of the renewal process, the Canadian operations of the bank, as mandated by the previous CEO, had retained a firm to conduct an employee engagement study and a company review. Over 90 percent of employees responded—an excellent response rate! The result would provide me with a great tool: I could get a clear snapshot of how the employees were feeling. The reality is that I had been quite detached from the Canadian side of the business as I had been working for ING Direct in the U.S. for over seven years and was very focused on the task at hand there.

Luckily, the questionnaire covered everything I felt was important. There was a series of questions on the workplace environment, and every answer helped me measure the likelihood of attaining our goals (and whether the employees even knew what those goals were). Before I embarked on reading the nearly 200-page document, I was grateful to have such a great guide.

What did the people say? Here are the 10 most important (for me) employee quotations from the final report:

1. I used to feel like a family at INGD, now I feel like a numbered employee.
2. People should be treated fairly. Favouritism is a big problem and should be avoided.

3. Our voices are not heard, instead brushed aside.
4. More than ever I feel INGD is turning into exactly what we don't want to become . . . our competition.
5. ING has failed me.
6. I am under pressure not to take time to do this survey.
7. All good employees are looking for and going to greener pastures elsewhere.
8. The environment is toxic and political, not to mention stressful.
9. I used to love coming to work.
10. This place has been like a rudderless ship for years.

"WHAT?!"

The most memorable feedback came from call centre staff. These are the people who speak with our clients day in, day out—the front door to our business, so to speak. Essentially they felt insignificant and they told us so, pointedly. They gave real examples, proof that what they said was true. Typically for most businesses, call centre associates are the least engaged employees. Their disengagement was devastating to me. In our vision for the business, our front-line staff needed to be the heroes, the most important and the most engaged of our employees. For ING Direct Canada to be a challenger their job satisfaction was a critical success factor. How had we lost track on this foundational element of who we were?

I wasn't even past page one before the report had my full, undivided attention. It was a touch depressing. Our overall engagement score was 58 out of 100. When I was in high school, 50 percent was the minimum passing grade, and today a pass is 60 percent. This was not good at all. It was failure. I was told that the average company scored 62 on the same test, but that was no comfort. Who cares? Who wants to say, "Well, we're no worse than the competition"? ING Direct was built on the foundation that we were a true challenger, and therefore we needed to be the best in certain areas. Having engaged, empowered employees was at the top of that list.

We weren't even average, and we'd set a lot higher goals than that. Some of the categories were more than just eye-openers, they were shocking. Here's what our employees thought about INGD at the time:

Team Quality, 49%; Team Collaboration, 44%; Team Trust, 47%. An entry in my personal notebook shows my take: "Traditional banking creeping in." No kidding.

In terms of how well we collaborated with each other—in other words, communication—44 percent could not pinpoint more than one thing that the bank was doing right, out of five choices. And our overarching corporate goals? Less than 28 percent of the workforce knew what our company goals were, and of those a whopping 3 percent knew how we measured success. *Three percent?* I am wary of getting caught up in numbers. Setting number-based targets can become a carrot-and-stick situation, where people blindly do anything to get the carrot. But when only 3 percent know that success means getting the carrot in the first place, you need to do something.

There were a few positive comments in the Free Comment sections, where people could write anonymously. Most respondents seemed nostalgic, wondering if we could ever recapture the feeling of pride in being different from, and better than, our competitors. They pointed out that:

- Communication was a huge problem: from departments to leaders to teams, everything was unclear.

- A developing, increasingly rigid hierarchy was holding things back.

- Favouritism was common and, even worse, nothing was being done to curb it.

- People were feeling automated at work.

- Most people had no idea of what other departments did, resulting in rivalries or mistrust.

- The lower down the ladder one went, individual quotas were set so high and allocated such tight deadlines that they became impossible to achieve.

- Morale was declining, because INGD was becoming "just another bank."

No matter how I assembled these facts, they told the same story, and it wasn't an INGD story. It was the opposite.

My feeling even before seeing this report was that we had become very conservative in culture and approach, which was pretty much in line with what I found in the survey. The left hand didn't know what the right hand was doing (not a good thing when both hands should be working together). Many of my impressions had now become measurable metrics. I put a lot of personal stock into things like trust, communication and honesty. According to these results, we had a lot of work to do.

It all had to do with human nature.

One thing to remember about people is that they like challenges. From a very early age, we instinctively crave structure, routine, discipline in some form, usually in the shape of tasks or goals. I don't think this changes as we get older—it just matures. I saw requests for more employee responsibility and autonomy, for the benefit of the company and the worker. Our people wanted to care, wanted to do something different and special again, wanted to challenge the status quo, and we were no longer giving them the chance.

I am a people-person. It was clear to me we needed a total refocus on our values. We needed to remake or refine our culture, who we were meant to be. By doing so, we could realign our machine and make it better than ever. In rowing, when everything is working perfectly, when the rowers are moving in synchronicity with each other, it is referred to as "swing." We needed to get our swing back so we could glide smoothly again.

There are two Chinese characters that make up the word *crisis*: they represent *risk* and *opportunity*. That is how I viewed this report, as an opportunity to give our employees exactly what they were missing, or hoping to obtain. The chance to build a better machine, one that can think and feel for itself.

A funny thing often happens when you hit rock bottom: your head cranes back up to where you came from, to where the light is.

Design a machine for human nature

You can't be an outlier unless you want to actually turn the tables upside down. —Arkadi Kuhlmann

When you watch the old footage on YouTube, it doesn't look like the game of soccer is about to change forever.

It's 1974 and the two best soccer teams in the world are about to face each other in the World Cup final. The band leaves the field. The legendary and punishing Franz Beckenbauer is in white and at the ready on the West German side. The magical goal-scorer Johan Cruyff, his hands resting on his hips, stares into the distance from the Dutch side of the ball. The rest of the players wait.

The referee stands with his arms crossed, waiting to signal the start of time . . . and then he blows his whistle. Cruyff pushes the ball to a teammate, who circulates it back to the rear. The ball moves up the middle and back to the Dutch defence. Then it's kicked up the left side before being redirected from the chasing Germans and back to Cruyff at midfield. The best forward in the world at this time, he's standing last on his own line of defence—and his team has the ball!

The field looks bigger and wider than usual, especially with the way the Netherlands taunts Germany with their neat passing, their natural shifting in and out of position. The Germans, meanwhile, tire of the chase and grow impatient. Suddenly *Cruyff gets the ball back*, just past midfield. He wanders forward and pushes neatly by a handful of defenders, and the moment he steps into the opposing team's scoring area, he's fouled before he can shoot at the net. The Dutch earn a penalty shot but Cruyff doesn't even take it—there's somebody better suited for the job.

The Netherlands scores. Every single member of the Dutch team touched the ball in the build-up. Not a single German player even touched a lace to the ball. Barely a minute had elapsed. It was the birth of what the Dutch called Total Football.

One person will tell you it took years of practice and perfecting, while another will say it took barely a minute . . .

The irony is that the Germans recovered from the shock, improvised with brutality, and won (how they won is still hotly debated and disputed to this day). Even though the Netherlands lost the game, they had completely changed the future direction, and therefore the history, of the world's most popular sport.

Total Football had a deceptively simple yet visionary concept at its core: any player could play any role on any part of the field, at any point in the game. Ten position players became interchangeable and could move in sync up and down the field. The slowest defender could score, the smallest forward could tackle. A player's job changed moment to moment, and that was the goal: to be ready for any situation, from every angle imaginable.

But what really made Total Football click was the way it was grounded in reality. Players didn't run all over chasing the ball; midfielders didn't suddenly play goalie; they were very aware that they had a specific role to play at any given moment. That the role could change from moment to moment had been anticipated. There was room in this fabulous machine for creativity and inspiration. For individuality.

The Germans were stunned, but after about 20 minutes they began to hammer the Dutch into submission. Not without skill and talent themselves, they scored two goals and won the final. They destroyed the amazing machine that had so badly embarrassed them at the start of the game. There are all sorts of theories as to how and why, but a big part was using brute strength.

Soccer has a conservative gatekeeper establishment, like most organizations. Success is often a matter of accepting that establishment, not making waves. The biggest problem for the Dutch was that the establishment was represented by three referees in black. They didn't have a choice, of course, except to take on the biggest powers on the biggest stage; but the laid-back, long-haired, freewheeling rebels didn't stand a chance.

When I think of Total Football and Tangerine, there are two things that stand out—one obvious and one not so obvious. Tangerine cultivates its people to be able to function anywhere on the field, like the Dutch team. This is evident and good, something we constantly strive for.

What we do about the gatekeepers is a little more subtle. Building the best machine meant, initially, changing the gatekeepers. We couldn't risk leaving power and rules in the hands of a small group, especially if our competitors were the ones who controlled the group. So we changed the rules to reflect what the public wanted—or better, what the public needed. With that in mind, we built a system that would change our rules with the changing needs of customers. Needs are in flux; our machine changes with them.

We have to be flexible, responsive, creative and inspired as employees. We have built these qualities into the architecture, and we have an algorithm that knows when to get out of a person's way when variations are called for. It enables us to listen to our clients and build our system around their real needs. Marketing can create artificial needs, but everything is so much clearer when you listen and respond to your clients with honesty.

Getting caught up in titles and narrow job descriptions kills creativity, nimbleness and response. Even if you need to build a machine, an operation that delivers profits, make sure the machine leaves room for people and gives them room to just be human, gives them room to work outside their box and allows them the freedom to be creative.

Listen to Frank Zappa

Without deviations from the norm, progress isn't possible.
—Frank Zappa

I remember a holiday staff party one Saturday night, to which we invited several of our employees' spouses, many of whom happened to work for our Big Bank competitors. At one point our guests started laughing at the way our people were interacting, their dress, their demeanour. "You would never see something like this where we are," one told me. "They'd never even get through the cafeteria. Only five years ago there was a woman who had an interesting job, if interesting means hard-to-believe. If you were having coffee or lunch and took your blazer off in the cafeteria, she'd tap you on the shoulder like a gruff old teacher and tell you to put your jacket back on."

He wasn't talking about the 1950s, but more than half a century later.

Obviously, that's not the kind of policy that would even be discussed, much less implemented, at Tangerine, but it carries important lessons. First of all, being different affects every part of the business, cafeteria included. Second, if you're going to look and behave differently, you have to think differently.

It would be easy here to talk about Steve Jobs and his "Think Different" motto, but someone already wrote that book so we'll refer to another kind of creative thinker, Frank Zappa. Although Zappa and his 1970s rock band The Mothers of Invention spilled a lot of controversial ink in newspapers over their careers (think "Bobby Brown Goes Down" and "Don't Eat the Yellow Snow"), they built legions of fans based on their musical creativity and Zappa's virtuoso genius. Zappa may have had children named Dweezil and Moon Unit, but he's also the guy who recorded albums of his own compositions with the London Symphony Orchestra. So when Zappa wrote, "Without deviations from the norm, progress isn't possible," I chose to listen.

This philosophy changed the way we plotted strategy and helped create a different working model. We saw that we couldn't take on the Big Five banks directly and win: they'd tap us on the shoulder and the blazer would have to come back on. We weren't going to beat the established banks at their game, on their turf, using their weapons. We had to change how the rules were written; the battleground and the weapons would then change as well.

We took the idea one step further. Our fight was about something much bigger. We were customer advocates. We were fighting for what we thought was in the best interest of Canadians, and we hoped to inspire Canadians to take action. To show their appreciation for us, or frustration with the status quo, and become our customers, our advocates, and of course bring their hard-earned savings into our strong, trusted arms.

By repeatedly opening that door to Canadians, we've let the majority be heard. Today, there is a clear demand for what most consumers need and want, not necessarily what the banks want.

In our hearts people see the world ideally, how we want to see it changed. We can afford to be idealistic there. If you want to transform you can't just improve on what already exists. You need to have a vision of how you want the world to be and find ways to make it happen. In our minds we know that change comes slowly, with a great deal of preparation. Setting winning conditions is as much mental as technical, and it is based in reality. You need the right mindset in every one of your employees going forward—like Total Football.

There is a pretty satisfying trajectory to the Total Football adventure: any serious soccer coach makes sure all the skills are learned by everyone, and any player can swap roles in an instant with another. If you don't agree, I highly recommend you watch the 2014 record-breaking season of FC Bayern Munich. In many ways, they owe more to the Dutch and Cruyff than to any German team before them.

Learn who you are by understanding who you're not

People don't know what they want until you show it to them.
—Steve Jobs

ING Direct Canada started in 1997, but even though we were desperate for customers, we couldn't handle customers calling us every day. The Internet wasn't prevalent when we launched (as the first ING Direct bank in the world), so everything we did was over the telephone. And because we were offering so much value, we knew people would say, "I want that savings rate!"

Customers went from wanting to talk with us to wanting to meet with us. They wanted to visit a branch. They wanted their idea of "direct" banking, which meant lineups, security guards and a vault. We would tell them: "We're a direct bank and you can't get into the habit of coming to see us." And they'd say: "I get it but I want to meet you just once. I'll give you my first cheque to open my account, I'll see you, and I promise I won't bug you again." People didn't understand that the bank had no physical space designed to meet our customers.

Our original building was a modest, low-cost 10-storey structure north of Toronto. When customers showed up there, we would take them into a waiting room they were never intended to see—a little foyer with nondescript grey carpeting. There was a wooden desk with a small ING Direct sign, and behind it sat Donna, our reception-ist. Behind her, a wall and 10 plain chairs. The interested customer would sit in the foyer, and then someone from the call centre would come in and do in person what he or she usually did over the phone.

We learned early on that this problem would have to be addressed. We told people they couldn't be served in person, that it wasn't our business model—but they didn't care. Some would drive two hours to see us. We were paying about five times on average what some other savings accounts paid, so in their minds it was worth the two-hour drive to see a bank employee deposit a cheque. If we allowed this to continue, we knew that customers would try to turn our only location into a more traditional branch, whereas we needed to demonstrate a new way of banking. We needed to re-engineer how our customers thought or we wouldn't survive.

And so we opened our first "Café." Its design did everything to avoid the look of a branch. No desks, no tellers, no person behind a counter, no lineup, no window, no pen with a chain. Every corner rounded off. There was no—bank! No money! None of the things people expect in a bank. Even today, if you hold up one of our Tangerine Cafés you'll get away with only coffee, cookies and a glass of freshly squeezed orange juice.

We had a mailbox in our first Café, and after clients had opened an account, we'd tell them: "Now go put your cheque in the mailbox over there, which you could have done without driving two hours to get here. And when you call us tomorrow, we'll tell you the money's in the account, earning interest." We decided to serve coffee (fair trade, of course) and call it a Café. If we didn't make it into something clear, customers would try to turn it into the only thing they knew: a branch. People turned the Café into whatever they wanted, except a bank branch. I remember people coming and wandering around aimlessly, because they weren't sure what to make of this non-branch of a non-bank.

I'll never forget the first day we opened. I watched a woman enter through the front door and take a look around, trying to find the spot for the lineup. She was totally lost.

If you need a branch, we're not the right bank for you. If you want to see your banker, look in the mirror. If you want to know your balance, look at your mobile phone or our web page. And if you get lost, call us and we'll always help you just enough until you can help yourself.

Offer customers slow-drip coffee, not espresso

We have to master the art of acting smaller as business gets bigger and moves that much faster. —@PeterAceto, December 9, 2013, Tweet

Coming home in 2008 was a bit of a nightmare, and not just because of the discouraging employee survey. I was alarmed to discover that the Cafés had become quite secondary and detached from the core business. No one had really explained (or understood) their initial purpose; there was no appreciation for the legacy—the entire situation was hugely disappointing. After all of our efforts, we'd lost something of our authenticity. Granted, there'd been a couple of different CEOs between the founder and me, and our styles varied greatly

To me, the Cafés were core to the business. I visited the Café in the head office building and witnessed an associate giving a client a little piece of paper. *What was that?* I wondered. No . . . it couldn't be . . . but yes, it was . . . a receipt! I couldn't believe my ears, my eyes. "We've been doing it for a long time," our Café associate told me about handing out paper receipts. She was trying to be helpful.

That's when I freaked out (in my head, initially).

Giving a customer a paper receipt missed the entire purpose behind our existence! Virtual and paperless. Period. Paper receipts were something we had decided never to do, in 1997, yet years later we were doing it? I was rather unpleased. We'd already had our moments of telling customers No when we'd tried to re-engineer their thinking about branches. Had we undone all of our great work?

Discovering the problem was indeed a nightmare, but a short-lived one, as it turned out. The staff responded straight away to the challenge of being consistent with our corporate promise. They knew giving receipts was wrong. Overnight, they stopped.

We wanted our process to be different from that of our competitors—we wanted it to be simple, all the time. I remember a customer visiting our first Café who was quite upset because we would no longer provide a paper receipt. I happened to be downstairs and helped our associate out. I explained why and suggested that maybe we were not the right bank for her. That if she needed to visit us regularly, and needed paper receipts and statements, she would be much better served by another bank. We did close her account, paid her every cent of interest owing and sent her money back to her other bank. This sent quite a message to our employees.

People can walk in off the street and use the Café whenever they want, to surf the Internet, read their papers, have a coffee, whatever. They don't have to be doing Tangerine-specific stuff; they may drop by because our sofas and chairs are really comfortable, or to sit and work at a beautiful table made of reclaimed wood. (Retail is detail, I have always believed.)

The Cafés are the physical manifestation of our brand. We need to be part of the community. Each Café has its own Twitter feed, and it speaks to what's going on locally, stuff that's germane to its particular area. This is marketing for us, allowing consumers to interact with the brand—like a 3-D interactive billboard—except it's in person. What people experience online or on the phone, here it can be felt and be real—and is totally different from what they're used to.

And yet the Cafés are the bank's lowest performers in terms of return on investment. In 2014, over 85 percent of what we do takes place on the Internet or on mobile devices: customer sign-up, buying banking products, doing transactions. The rest mostly takes place in our contact centres via phone, and a small proportion occurs in one of our five physical locations.

The concept has constantly changed because of all kinds of learning. Café 2.0 in the U.S. was all about coffee. We sold thousands and thousands of cups of coffee. Our coffee was a dual metaphor for our business: we serve really great coffee at an affordable price, just like our products, and banking can be as easy and painless as getting a cup of coffee.

At our New York Café, people lined up out the door. They wanted an excellent, inexpensive, friendly cup of coffee as they walked to work. Our Café associates made a mean cup of coffee, but who wants to talk about savings, retirement, buying a home or investments with a barista? The great value and service on display were a perfect reflection of our core values, but we needed to slow it down a bit. The problem was that the coffee didn't take long enough to make, not long enough to have a useful conversation about banking. We learned from that. It became less about volume of traffic and more about quality of interaction between our employees, our space and the people who came through the door.

All we had to do was change how we made coffee. To give people a chance to chat for a minute, about whatever. Because at some point, the chat will turn to banking. But if you need a coffee in two seconds and haul off to work, our Cafés are not the place and not the time.

As I write this, we are on the eve of testing a new concept to complement our Cafés. We call them our "mobile pop-ups." Imagine a beautifully renovated shipping container showcasing a never-before-seen client sign-up experience. The jury is out, but we are excited about bringing this leap forward to Canadians.

Don't sell, help

Customer service isn't a strategy.
—@PeterAceto, November 11, 2013 Tweet

It's so achingly simple but so few people seem to get it. Stop selling products. Be there to assist your customer, but just give them some room. People everywhere are sick and tired of getting a hard sell. With little choice and increasing pressure to buy things they don't need, people get deflated and depressed. We are all consumers and we all hate being sold stuff.

I guarantee you that if you come to one of our Cafés for a coffee once a week, at some point you'll ask us about our business and probably become a customer. We don't push it; instead we try to create a relaxed atmosphere that's engaging. And the coffee's never free—it's just good value. It's also a physical touch point with our brand. We don't want to scream at people all day with marketing. People have to understand that Tangerine is different. They come first for the coffee and to interact with our brand, and over time they see how we are different (sometimes five minutes, sometimes five months). Eventually a deeper relationship is formed.

It costs a lot of money to operate the Cafés, but one discussion the bank has never had is how to make them profitable. The finance team asks a lot of questions about cost benefit, as well it should, but we make sure we know how to define the actual benefit beyond straight numbers.

I can't take the cost of the Cafés and divide by the number of new clients we get from them and show you a return that is better than any other marketing that we do. But I can show you that the nature of the interaction and of the customer we get there far exceeds the typical bank's customer base. Our clients who started at our Cafés often become ambassadors for our brand. This place is transformational, and there's something special about the interactions. They become customers, they buy more products, and they tell people about us.

I don't pay our Café staff per customer won or per product sold. No commission.

Everyone in our company has goals, and how they do against those goals has a lot to do with their performance review and compensation. We hire people who love us, who love our business and their jobs, and who believe in us. We love and believe in them right back. They are genuine, and that transfers to their interactions with the people who walk into a Café off the street.

How complicated is that?

Have a Guinness when you're tired

Guinness Is Good for You. —1929 advertising slogan

Guinness is a well-known international company that has implemented some interesting people-policies over the years. I'll get into the why in a moment, but here are some of their innovative ideas.

It started in the early 1900s with organized athletic and cultural clubs for employees, when Guinness built a gymnasium and a swimming pool. It developed a loans and savings division for staff, with a mortgage section that arranged low-interest loans so that people could become owners instead of tenants and build long-term value. Later, by buying and building on most of the land around their centre of operations, the company was able to offer some workers low-rent housing.

That wasn't it. Visits to the hospital and extended stays in hospices were covered, and Guinness would pay from two-thirds to all of your salary if you got too sick to work. There were free medical services, dental services, and medicine for workers and their families. On staff was a small team of doctors, nurses, chemists and even a masseuse, all free to visit.

The brewer paid above-market rates for all jobs and offered the security of lifetime employment, preferring to teach and train instead of fire. Young workers were encouraged to attend trade and technical schools—tuition expenses paid—and were rewarded for great exam results. For a long time the corporate pension plan was run entirely by the company: employees did not have to pay into it at all. Guinness covered funeral expenses and made sure, in tough times and tough neighbourhoods, that kids of deceased workers would get free meals, and widows a continuing pension. On days off, managers encouraged their employees to escape the city with their families, picking up the tab for train tickets and other expenses.

On top of all that, Guinness offered employees—and still does today—a daily partaking of the one and only flagship product: two pints of Guinness Stout.

Remarkably, every one of those policies was in place by 1900. So, well over a century ago, someone at Guinness realized that to build up their formidable business machine, they had to put their people first, be they barrel-builders or executive clerks.

Today Guinness brews over 1.8 billion pints a year, operating in 60 countries and selling in more than 100 nations. For numbers like those, you have to have built a very sophisticated machine capable of micro and macro processing, but also able to change. It's intricate and depends on a lot of moving parts. Guinness has international distribution and localized manufacturing, an iconic marketing/PR tradition, innovative branding, huge penetration into the global market, and an emotional and physical bond—maybe unprecedented—with its consumer base. It also rolled out one of the greatest advertising campaigns of all time: "Guinness Is Good for You." The slogan can be looked at in a couple of ways: first, that there are possible health benefits to downing a pint or two a day and, second, that the company is active in taking care of its employees.

Why does any of this interest a bank CEO? For one, not all the best ideas come from my desk. History is pretty useful if you can take the good points and leave the bad behind. Tangerine is not going to conform its machine to the 1900 version of Guinness, but we can see a lot of great ideas in the formative stages of this incredibly powerful business and brand. How they built that vital machine, through the needs of their people, is pertinent.

The most amazing thing is that Guinness had absolutely no incentive to do any of this stuff. None. Guinness was already far and away the biggest brewery in the world, backed by a massive 10 percent market share in England. They were more than doubling the production and sales of their nearest competitor. When they went public, their stock price rose 60 percent on the first day. And all this without owning a single pub or spending a black penny on advertising.

So why bother? Britain was still very much in the clutches of the industrial age, where the worker was seen as the lowest rung on the ladder, disposable, replaceable, underpaid and undervalued. I like to think that early on, someone at Guinness recognized the cost of great value. Their stout wasn't the cheapest drink on the market, but it was the best value. You could rely on a great, consistent product as well as on innovative new ones.

The cost for Guinness lay in building and maintaining a loyal and proud workforce, from the guys building the barrels to the captains of their shipping fleet; from the women working the lunchroom to the board and the senior clerks. They wanted a body of employees that not only enjoyed working at Guinness but also saw opportunities to create even better products, an even stronger company, and a better sense of their own worth.

Guinness didn't cultivate that loyalty through free beer: They wanted an educated, solvent, secure and happy workforce. They wanted people to get and stay healthy. They wanted better minds from the ground up, or from the cobblestones up, as it was then. They wanted their people and their clients to understand the difference between cost and value. Oscar Wilde, another Irishman who might have enjoyed a couple of pints, may have said it best: "What is a cynic? A man who knows the price of everything and the value of nothing."

In 1907 employee welfare plans cost Guinness 40,000 pounds a year, which was one-fifth of their wage bill. A few cuts here and there would have meant a nice propping-up of the bottom line. Back then not many would have complained about a regression to the norm: the employees saw themselves as very fortunate to begin with. But Guinness knew that happy, innovative, loyal people paid out much more than numbers in the long run. That was how they built such an ambitious machine, by putting their people first.

I wonder how many companies today can match what Guinness was doing over 100 years ago. While things have changed, Guinness hasn't abandoned all its ground-breaking principles. It closed the Dundalk brewery a little while ago, the first plant they have ever shut down, but offered the 140 people laid off free private health care, scholarships for their kids, payouts to last at least a year, and 14 bottles of Guinness a week for 10 years.

I've always believed in the importance of putting people first. When it came time to rework the machine at ING, we had a lot of options and a lot of ideas. But I knew that the machine would have to reflect my core values, which are directly aligned with the company's core values. And the foundation for those values was always going to be putting our people first.

So we had to build a machine out of people, loyalty, pride, ambition: a human machine, not one of only nuts and bolts and interest rates and profit margins. A machine built that way would undoubtedly benefit people above everything else. By putting personal values into place in the company, and remembering the values set down by our founders, I knew we were working toward something that would put everyone in a better place: shareholders, employees, customers, community.

If Guinness is good for you, why not Tangerine, too? I don't often drink, but I'll drink to that.

Pick a colour

Anyone can start something new. It takes real leaders to
stop something old. —@PeterAceto, February 12, 2014, Tweet

One of the most fantastic athletes and champions in the world of sport is a mixed martial artist from St-Isidore, Quebec, named Georges St-Pierre. When he entered semi-retirement in 2014, GSP (as his fans call him) had accumulated the best statistical record of any fighter in the history of his sport. The best punching numbers. The top-rated defence. And, perhaps most importantly, more title defences and rounds as a world champion than anyone else, ever.

What makes Georges St-Pierre so strong is knowing what makes him weak. His entire system is based on a martial arts technique he invented called shoot-boxing. The way it works is simple: Georges identifies your weakness and directs the fight toward it so that you are never in your comfort zone, and always in his. Because mixed martial arts is a compendium of fighting disciplines, the key is being good at a variety of fighting styles. GSP may not be the best wrestler in the world, but he can outpunch and outkick most wrestlers, so he will fight them standing. Or, if he's fighting an opponent who has neglected his jiu jitsu, GSP will take him to the ground and, most likely, force him to submit, thanks to his superior technical ability on the ground.

In other words, he decides where the fight takes place, and that's how he builds an advantage. The way he has done it is simple: perfect as many martial arts as possible. He started the process when he was seven years old. That's why he's often been so far in front of the competition and has remained there—by being elusive and knowing all the techniques (not just the tricks) in the book. GSP's genius comes from routine simplicity, combined with once-in-an-era talent, to achieve a clear goal: become the best martial artist the world has seen. The ideal of simplicity is one I have also tried to incorporate into my professional life. Entries scribbled in my notebooks over the years illustrate this goal:

"Be easy."
"Be simple."
"Help people be smart."
"Simplify financial products."
"Lead people to saving money."
"Only offer smart, easy-to-use choices."

These simple phrases were strewn among dull, technical reminders and meeting report lists, popping up on the pages of my medium-sized black books, among the thoughts I recorded during my last year of residence in the U.S. When they're read in succession, they begin to form the core of a bigger idea. The key is implementing the idea across the company from the very beginning. Just like building an important structure, everything rests on the columns of a deep foundation. These columns are the principles I had been discovering, reflecting on and refining for years—all connected to the overarching principles of the company.

It was good to review these values (and *those notebooks!*) because they pointed in a direction that would re-establish our brand as a challenger, especially in comparison to the Big Five. Change was necessary because we had been slipping towards the business culture and practices of the competition. We were beginning to fight them on their terms, and if we pursued, it wasn't going to end well or be pretty.

It's simple: Tangerine cannot compete with the Big Five on their terms. It's why, from the outset, we were set up to be different and to fight battles differently, choosing new front lines. Sure, we competed with them, but we had to compete our way and create our own category of expertise.

Upon my return from the U.S., I knew the machine needed improving. If you know your machine needs fixing and you understand that it is run on human power, then the ability to work honestly and in open communication is what allows for change. Tweak how the machine thinks, the process will adapt, and the output will change.

It was clear to me and many others that we had to rebuild trust, re-engage our workforce and be transparent. Our audience wasn't just on the outside, they were on the inside, wondering what was happening to their company. And these were the people operating the machine.

I saw this moment as a great opportunity, a chance to do something good for the company and earn some respect (and therefore trust) from my colleagues. In business relationships, as in life, we can't accomplish much if we don't find ways of trusting each other: trust that we have the confidence of the company behind us; trust that we are moving in the right direction; trust that we are empowered and will be rewarded for good results. Communication goes in both directions, but people have to feel comfortable addressing challenging, stressful issues. This is a key principle for me, a pillar, and in spirit, it's the centrepiece of the vision.

This is how I concluded my first speech as CEO to the employees: "I need two things from all of you: your attentiveness to our customers, and your honesty and candour. Please speak to or email me directly." It wasn't lip service, telling people to speak to me or email me. I was, and still am, accessible (within limits of course). But communication starts from the top.

The good thing about having studied psychology in university is that it taught me something about people: we want to feel good about ourselves. That means my job is to create a culture that helps people feel good about their work, that makes their work meaningful. Essentially, happy in their work. Establishing trust and respect from the get-go makes it a standard across the company that applies to everybody. If I wanted our employees to become our brand ambassadors, I had to lead them there. Inside the bank we'd actually given this a name. We called it "Being Orange."

So when I said that we had gotten away from being ourselves, from what made us different, I said we had moved away from Being Orange. I remember heads nodding. Everybody got it. I also remember smiling because we knew we were about to turn another corner.

Making genuine connections generates commitment. This in turn forms a strong corporate culture. Talking to the senior staff, it became clear there were some who earnestly believed in using passion as part of their daily working lives and some who were short of ideas and motivation, who weren't interested in pushing the needle.

Leaders need to be extensions of our guiding principles. If we could get that kind of leading team, then energize our people to feel the way we did, extending that respect to customers would become an everyday thing. Again it came down to people power. People are a business's greatest asset, not money.

And so we picked a colour—orange—and defined what it means to Be Orange. We created a plan, stuck to it, and then repeated it consistently across all operations. To give meaning to Being Orange.

Some employees were still getting real results. There was still passion involved, and certainly dedication. Employees were longing for the things that once separated us from other banks. Many of our staff still excelled under pressure. You can't throw the baby out with the bath water.

I knew people had pride in our difference. To get back to being different in a meaningful way, and give people back a sense of pride in themselves and their employer again, we had to remove the following negative factors:

- silo focus in departments
- being overly humble
- poor rewards for performance
- unfair promotions
- a focus on the past, not the present
- an aversion to risk
- dishonest spin messaging

We know we are constantly building a system to fit the people, giving them room for expression and risk. We aren't building people to fit an inflexible system.

We just get to pick the colour.

Be realistically idealistic

The art of life is a constant readjustment to our surroundings.
—Kakuzo Okakura

Franz Kafka is said to have uttered this wonderful line: "In the battle between you and the world, back the world."

Like all great sayings that inspire me, I've applied the thinking to Tangerine. It's true, by aiming to become so different from all other banks and financial institutions out there, we are unique. But at what cost? If we decided to apply a series of drastic changes to banking overnight, we would indeed be different, but we could easily wind up isolated.

It's the difference between the leading edge and the bleeding edge: careful balance is needed, because if you get too far ahead you'll get arrows in the back. Worse, you'll be out of touch and impractical, irrelevant.

I wake up at least once a week with an idea, and admittedly many of them are a bit out there. I'd drive everyone crazy if I marched in every time a new idea came to me and shouted, "We gotta get on this now!" We need to choose with discretion. Same with helping Canadians change their financial habits. We can move people along, but only so fast. You have to apply a certain degree of pragmatism to any viable dream.

Change may be constant, but you need to measure its speed.

While many initiatives are idealistic and aim to change the world, they must be executed with the consumer top of mind—that's all that matters. In other words, when fighting decades-old habits, while our aim may be altruistic, our process has to be realistic. You can't throw your consumers into the deep end and expect them to swim. Here's a concrete example.

In the U.S., we launched a product that we called Electric Orange. In banking language it was a chequing account, but it looked quite different. It was paperless—a chequing account with no cheques. We wanted to create a totally new category or at least not be defined by the way people categorize products, so we did not call it a chequing account. It was ground-breaking, a revolution in our industry. A great idea, connected to a great vision.

Although we were very proud of Electric Orange, we did not see the results we had hoped for. Consumers told us that they didn't know what an "electric orange" was or why they would want or need it. Even once they understood, they insisted that they still sometimes needed physical cheques. Although some customers did choose to purchase the product, it did not have the game-changing mass appeal that it could have delivered. Visionary, yes. Beautiful, yes. Game changing, no.

When we launched a similar product in Canada, THRiVE Chequing (which, ideally, would also be 100 percent paperless), we included paper cheques, and still do. We also used the word *chequing* in the name. As of 2014, it is the chequing account with the best ratio of paper to electronic transactions in Canada. We received a prestigious award for it as well. Our customers love that they can be very close to their money at all times. They do most of their payments with their mobile phones, debit cards, free email money transfers—and yes a cheque here and there. Our goal was to create the chequing account with the highest ratio of electronic payments to paper payments in the industry. We needed the paper cheques to get customers to try us, and we engineered the product so paper was not the best way to use the account. Giving consumers the option of paper or electronic leads to their telling others, which leads to increasing sales, which is the point. In fact, our customers are among our best salespeople for this product.

I get sticking to your guns, and having a vision and keeping it pure. But in business, you need to keep your dream alive, to realize it may take a step or two to bring people along. Every vision needs pragmatism and a real-world working approach to achieve it. Sooner or later, there will be 100 percent paperless chequing in Canada, and we will make it happen.

Ideally, we would have loved for everyone to go paperless from the get-go, but the reality is that this kind of change has to simmer a little longer. Do I ask myself if I sold out? Could I have been bolder, more visionary? Maybe. Time will tell. I am certain that I am always at least a little wrong but you've got to stick with it. Make adjustments, tweaks and changes along the way.

As long as idealism has a dose of pragmatism, good will come from it.

Imperfect is perfect enough

Beware, perfection gets in the way of success.
—@PeterAceto, November 4, 2013, Tweet

How far along does an idea have to be for me to give it the green light? The truth is that a lot of it is just gut feeling. This might surprise some, but you have to respect that the machine you create has a built-in place for feelings, or instinct as some might say.

The rule I've read in many books is that, when you feel 80 percent certain, go. But I like challenges, so if most people would say launch at 80 percent done, I'll usually ask for 90. I'll always raise that extra 10 percent because I'm confident our model, our employees (and our active customers, always willing to contribute to make our products better) will come closer to a perfect product, in a shorter time, than any of our competitors.

Anyone can agree that there's a fine balance between Perfectionism and Getting It Done. I've met people who are perfectionists, and they rarely get anything done. Perfectionism is a detrimental condition, with obsessiveness over small details and stubbornness. People get afraid, become frustrated, abandon projects. They're trying to create a 100 percent risk-free environment, which is not realistic, especially in financial services—especially for a challenger like Tangerine.

If you are the big player in the market, the tendency is to defend yourself. Be safe, don't cause problems, don't take risks. After all, the status quo was created by you and works for you. Why rock the boat? But if you are the predator hunting the big guys down, you need to move, take risks, and never get tangled up shooting for perfection.

Arkadi Kuhlmann could often be a bit of a perfectionist—which is both good and bad. When we first started out with an idea of a different way to do your banking, Arkadi had a vision—an ideal—to present something different. But visions are like statues: over time, people chip away at them, eroding the ideal you started off with. In the early days of the bank, the chipping came often: you can't *not* hire bankers because the regulator won't take you seriously, you *can't* call yourself this or that because nobody else does it that way, and on and on. It became tiresome.

Financial services is arguably the most conservative industry going, and here were a bunch of newbies—not all of them bankers—trying to completely change the way to do business, through innovation and new perspectives. What a task! Through it all, the founder kept to the stick-to-it-ness of his vision, even though it was constantly being chipped at. The thing about all that chipping is that, when you are well managed, the chips just hit your surface. They don't get to the core.

You need two kinds of knowledge to be a business leader: understanding the theory and then applying it (usually by breaking the rules, yours included). The best journalists looking to write a column know the history, the theory, the ethics, the philosophy and the technique, but they still need to tell a story.

This is something I grapple with because I am the guy who chooses when to stop tinkering with something and launch it into the marketplace. My inner nature wants to succeed, and I want things to be perfect. So how do I make that choice? How do I delegate the key tasks? How good does it need to be before I sign off?

The answers aren't in metrics or stats or even in a CEO's authority. Timing has something to do with it, but basically it's a leadership issue. (Leadership books are too short, by the way. You don't want to read it if it's too long, but leadership is too complicated to explain in a 20-page chapter or with a few broad concepts.) If something needs to be perfect to launch in the marketplace, then it probably won't ever get there.

You need to hear all the arguments, assess your feelings, and move forward. Experience mixes with instinct. You can't be too weighed down by the technical arguments against; you can't get carried away by the excitement of arguments for, either. It also depends on your ability to read and react. If you are nimble, you know you can make adjustments quickly when needed. Get the product into the customers' hands and adjust as you go. If you can't do that, you'd better nail it the first time, which is nearly impossible.

By structuring room for creativity into the architecture of your machine, you allow people to use their skills and emotions when doing business. Head and heart, everything is a balancing act. There are biases, but this is a business, and business needs to move forward.

Decision making and motion are deeply connected.

Just tell me what you're good at

No man will make a great leader who wants to do it all himself or get all the credit for doing it. —Andrew Carnegie

I am not making this up: a good friend of mine lies to his clients and colleagues because it's the only way he gets to do what he's good at. He's an ideas guy, a creative leader who has developed ideas worth millions of dollars for his companies over the years. But he doesn't want anything to do with managing the money or the people. So he lies. He says things like: "If you want to talk about the retainer or the budget, I'll get you the right person. If you want to lose all your money, let me manage it." This scares clients into seeking the money people, but it also ensures that he focuses on what he likes doing, which also happens to be what he's best at.

Now, he knows how to count. He knows how to manage teams of 35 to 50 people because he's done it and proven himself. But he also happens to know that he's on a team, and that there are other people on the team who are much better at Excel spreadsheets and much worse at finding and developing ideas.

His little white-lying actually benefits everybody: The client is thrilled to have a strong ideas person and relieved to meet the budget and team manager. The team manager wins because she or he feels valued and makes a contribution. And the little white liar wins because everybody else is happy—him included.

The machine wins, too, because the parts are being used to their original design and intent. This is not the norm.

When I returned to Canada, I discovered that certain people were taking all the opportunities to speak in key meetings while others just sat there, silently. They'd been told, or sensed, that they should keep their mouths shut. Just because it says VP on your job description, do you get to talk and a director doesn't? We're all "associates" when we walk into a room for a meeting, and I want all ideas and voices to be heard no matter where they come from. Eliminate the hierarchy. Nothing screams hierarchy more than job titles on business cards.

We have never had titles on business cards or on email signatures. Everyone at Tangerine has a job description with the goal of providing clarity and accountability. However, employees also have permission and are indeed expected to reach out further and broader than the words written on a piece of paper. Clarity and accountability are absolutely required, but job descriptions are artificial and can be extremely limiting. We are lateral thinkers, problem solvers: these are the people we need to take us further.

A job title on a card is an element of traditional hierarchy from the past. We don't want to be there. When an employee is in a meeting, she's the leader of our business, our ambassador, and I expect her to behave that way whether she's got the big title or not. Vice president, manager, who cares? A partner or a vendor will soon figure out that he is sitting across from the representative for our company, the best person we can send for that meeting.

I don't know what the title is that fits my job description. I can't put a title on it. My accountant, the insurance guy and even the government don't get it. It doesn't mean anything. What's always been more important to me is to find the right way to tell a story. If you're a customer, I'll find the right way to tell your story. Who cares that I'm a CEO?

If it says you've done something on your CV, why would I check your core competencies? It says you know how to program, analyze, whatever. I'm okay with that—I start every relationship at a full tank on the trust meter. And if you can't do what's on your CV, I will find out and soon.

I'd rather look at people, not paper. If the system only worked on paper, most of my staff—me included—would be doing something else. I don't want to talk about organizational charts and who reports to whom. Hierarchies have always been outside our philosophy, as much as possible. Increasingly, the worldwide trend in business is moving away from hierarchies. I think we are ahead of the curve.

Every year an employee comes to me and asks to revisit the issue around titles on business cards, etc., and every year I listen, and every time I absolutely refuse. We don't have titles on our business cards, and that's that. This causes some issues around clarity and accountability; but how does a little line on an organizational chart solve big issues? It doesn't.

John Wooden, the influential basketball coach at UCLA, said, "It is amazing how much can be accomplished if no one cares who gets the credit." Working hard just to achieve a title is just another form of seeking credit. My approach to work and people is this: Why don't we work together, you and me, and get the job done? Be open, honest and flexible.

In some cultures or industries, you have to know who's No. 1, who's No. 2, who's No. 3. In my view, you're a person: Just say what you're responsible for. Tell me what you're good at. And if you want to, tell me what you don't do, don't know and aren't good at. When our people say *I'm responsible for the products in the bank, or I'm running our channels*, they aren't tying themselves to a general title without specifics. It's in their nature not to get caught up in titles and descriptions.

People do like to go home to their loved ones, their parents, their friends, and say, "Look what just happened: I'm the CEO of that, or the manager of this." I get it. It's easy for me to insist on no titles as the person in charge, and we do have people heading our various departments. If you want to put your title on your CV or tell your family, I don't care—but I don't want it on the bottom of your email. It sends the wrong message.

If we have this discussion in 2025 I might have a different view of some of the things I've done, but I don't give up on my core beliefs or decisions because I read something different in a book.

I don't even give out my business card anymore. Give me your card and I'll send you my ecard with a nice message.

Theory is (sometimes) only good in theory

The minute you make it about yourself, you lose credibility and you lose trust. —@PeterAceto, February 3, 2014, Tweet

There's a running gag related to the *New York Times* and founder Adolph Ochs's mantra, which has appeared at the top of the front page every day since 1898. Ochs demanded "All the news that's fit to print," while reporters joke it should be "All the news that prints to fit."

The nuance is important. Choosing news that is fit to print is the job of an editor. Fitting the news into a delineated print format is the job of a graphic designer. Knowing the difference is the job of a . . . well, whose job is it? Good question.

When I was at law school, lawyers would regularly come in and teach a class, and the most interesting lectures were delivered by practitioners as opposed to actual professors. It was clear even then that I was already more interested in real life over theory. And in the real world, you need people suited to the task at hand. They may not be an expert in a specific area of business, but we see top, very dynamic people shift industries all the time.

Some industries lag far behind. Universities, for example, usually hire PhDs to run schools and not businesspeople (although a few schools have tried to change this). But tenured professors freak out if the suggestion is made to turn over the operations to a business-first person, even though a university doesn't run on theory. By hiring an academic to do a business job, you may as well have a textbook running a school. There's an ingredient that's missing: reality.

Some of the most successful coaches in the history of sport were not high-performance athletes. They could draw Xs and Os, but they couldn't walk onto a court or ice surface and execute—they needed athletes to do so. Some of the best legal offices in the world have adopted the trend of having a CEO who is not a law practitioner or expert. They can talk turkey, but not in Latin, and not before a judge. And some of the most interesting restaurants in the world are run by people who can't actually cook, who can't bake, and who aren't any good at clearing tables.

Why is that? It's because these businesses have something in common: sales. They make sales. And sales means consumers making buying decisions, which means service. This means service comes first.

The core of Tangerine's business is our clients. The customers come first. When I came back as CEO, we made changes. We weren't reinventing the wheel but getting back to the basic tenets of the bank's founders. There is nothing more real than someone who wants to balance a budget or save money. We de-emphasized hierarchies and organizational charts and went back to the simple root of our brand, which is above all customer advocacy. Our customers own and define our brand. Who we are.

Most established large companies have been geared around what the company wants: to sell a mortgage, to have everyone who walks through the doors buy five products in a certain amount of time, to increase the consumer base at all costs. The starting point in our operation is different: It's about a person who's making the biggest purchase in his or her life and how we want to be part of that process. It's about a person trying to save money for some very important life goal or objective and how we run the best business there is to help people do just that.

When it comes down to it, people don't want to bank. They want to live happy lives today and in the future. They want to be able to purchase stuff, take care of their needs, have fun and save for their future. We want to help them with these things, that's all. Our machine, putting employees first and fuelling it with the clients' needs, is the most realistic business model for a bank. And it is timeless, based on things that will always be important: helping our clients live a happy, healthy life.

Put people first and your bottom line will reflect their loyalty. Put your bottom line first and you are forever fighting battles against yourselves, and you'll be forced to lose alignment with your clients.

Not all industries follow this approach.

The newspaper business is a good example. Being in the media this century is about more than covering news. It's an evolving, ever-shifting business, and some organizations still haven't adapted.

Be a reporter who gets great scoops and exclusive stories, and you'll be promoted to columnist. Sure, you'll get your headshot in the paper and your personal opinion in the news, but are you a good writer? Or still just a good reporter? The idea sounds good, but reporting the facts is quite different from expressing a point of view on the evolution of society in 800 entertaining words.

My idea is this: Theory is great if it serves the customer first and you second. If it's the other way around, you win, but the customer disappears, and so, you really lose.

Get your customers to work for you

You need a clear view about your business's capabilities before making promises to customers. —@PeterAceto, November 4, 2013, Tweet

If you have a beautiful idea but you have no way of realistically attaining it until consumers find it useful, then you need consumers to take the lead. They will own the product and contribute to making it better, more useful to them. Paperless chequing is a brilliant concept, but we knew it needed a little real-world tweaking; and who better to make those suggestions than the people who would use it and benefit the most from it?

Before launching THRiVE Chequing, we offered the new product for free to 20,000 of our existing customers, mostly people who had volunteered to be the first beta testing group. It was ready for the marketplace but needed real feedback from the people who would use it every day. It wasn't perfect, but it was marketplace-ready. You can't wait forever trying to perfect something before getting it into your customers' hands, and you can't give them something too vague. Telling our customers that THRiVE was in a test phase gave us the right to make a few mistakes. Nonetheless, 20,000 customer-testers lined up virtually to get the product. They knew they were going to be the first people to use it, and one of their obligations was to tell us what could be better about it.

We got a tremendous amount of feedback, from concrete criticisms to "I wish this were better." We made hundreds of changes based on what our clients wanted and needed. We said no to many things, too. People will try to turn things into what they know, which is why Steve Jobs never asked what Apple's customers wanted. If you put it out there, you've got to be prepared to listen, and sometimes say no.

We relied on our client base and, by giving them the responsibility to provide feedback, we gave them pride in and ownership of the product. Essentially they were working for free, but we didn't look at it that way. They were helping to make this new banking product better for themselves.

Don't hire servers for a buffet

It is not the strongest or the most intelligent who will survive but those who can best manage change. —Charles Darwin

When I compare Tangerine to the competition, I envision a bunch of elephants shuffling along, with a little energetic orange beast nimbly moving and dancing at their feet.

The typical bank in this country has over 1,000 branches. The overhead is significant, which means that someone has to pay for it (guess who?). Heck, that's more buildings than Tangerine has staff! Our cost of doing business is a fraction of this. We're quick, mobile, nimble and definitely flexible. We have to use our smaller size to our advantage, we must dance around their feet, and we must be faster. We're not so small anymore and we're getting bigger, but we're keeping that mindset. We need to.

It means, though, that there are rules to get into the dance. We want a customer who'll do a bit more work on her own. We need a self-directed customer, willing to help himself. Customers willing to do so will be richly rewarded—that's essentially our business model. Whether clients are on their mobile devices, on the telephone or online, the banking process is essentially the same, and we don't treat people differently whether they're richer or poorer. The only measure that interests us is growth. The interest rates are the same for everybody, regardless of their account balances. This approach allows us to be simple and keeps our costs extremely low. We can share a portion of our savings with customers by eliminating fees while providing higher interest on their savings.

We don't want customers to open accounts and then come back every week to get us to do something for them. That's not our service model. We stick to our 80-20 rule: we can't let 20 percent of our clients create 80 percent of the work, or the model breaks. We need to catch the right fish, and if we pull one in that isn't right, back into the water it goes. Without this discipline, we will not be around to keep fishing for very long.

Knowing which customers are right for our model means we need to understand which are not right for us. Marketers understand this concept well and spend part of their time thinking about customer segments—how different groups of people are similar, what their needs/wants are and how to serve them. We have a unique way of segmenting consumers. It's not about postal code or region; it has little to do with geography or affluence. We don't work that way and don't need to. We actually don't want everybody.

In the early years after launching the bank, the biggest surprise was that many senior citizens became customers. We didn't think ours was the kind of banking experience they would appreciate. We thought they would prefer the traditional bank branch experience. When asked, their typical reply can be summed up as: *I may be old but I'm not stupid. I know good value when I see it.* Luckily, our machine knows how to listen and adapt, so it did.

Our focus on client demographics is based entirely on the actual needs of people and on products that can fulfil those needs. We know we can't be all things to all people, and we know that we'll never try to be. Overextending yourself, over-committing, is setting yourself up to fail. We profile our customers. We build archetypes. We look at our millions of customers and look at the kind of people they are. Other banks are branch-centric, and our customer doesn't need a branch with all the trappings. Laptop, smartphone, tablet—there's your branch. And you are the teller.

As a result, we have clients—evangelists—who spread the good word about us and are often our most efficient sales force. It was important to us that we reward these brand ambassadors. So, every year we send out a branded soccer-style scarf to 365 people who engage with clients, who are active in social media channels on our behalf. We call this our Orange Scarf Ambassador program. We also reward clients when they refer a friend or family member to our business. Our Orange Key referral program has been our most successful client acquisition tool in our history.

Tangerine's customers are like people at a buffet—the food is set out for them, but they get their own plates and choose their own dessert.

See victory through your clients' eyes

In the late 2000s, the Canadian government announced that it was going to create a new way for people to save money, tax-free—the Tax-Free Savings Account (TFSA). For the government it was just good policy, following in the footsteps of Registered Retirement Savings Plans (RRSPs), launched in 1957, which helped Canadians save money while deferring taxes. The TFSA was not designed to help just wealthy Canadians but to help all Canadians at all stages of their savings careers.

I remember sitting in a meeting room with my team and a flock of consultants who were outlining how they thought this new program would work. They did not paint an encouraging picture. The consultants told us that TFSAs would only be "defensive products." Banks would offer them to retain their customers and their savings and investments—nothing more. Clearly, bankers could not grow their business using TFSAs. In their eyes the TFSA wasn't a game-changer or a differentiator.

These "experts" were mistakenly looking at this new product through the lens of the financial industry, their own banking industry, and not through the lens of the consumer. They had no regard for how or if TFSAs might be beneficial to consumers, and there was little talk of how these new accounts could be exploited to benefit both consumers and banks. I vividly remember sitting in that room and thinking: "This is the biggest freaking opportunity we've ever had, and it's just fallen into our laps. This is incredible, and these consultants are going around telling everybody not to worry about it. *Holy crap!*"

I called a meeting with my team for later that day. We weren't waiting on this one, consultants be damned. The announcement by the government came with very short notice for the financial industry. They told us they were launching the program in six months. My team and I knew that we had to drop everything and build this capability. So we quickly had a cross-functional meeting to get our leaders' feedback and begin planning. After initial discussions, our team came back and said they agreed. In fact, they went even further. We would begin to build the TFSA business immediately, and they had a very interesting proposition.

TFSAs wouldn't formally exist in law until January 1, 2009, but the team proposed launching INGD's own version in October, three months prior to the official date. The mandated tax benefit would only start in January, but INGD would give the tax benefit to Canadians who signed on with us before that date. Our message would be: *The taxman isn't going to help you until January 1st, but we will help you now.* Our way of giving that benefit to our customers was by doubling their interest rate until January 1, when the taxman would step in with the tax incentive. Double the interest!

On top of that, we repurposed all of our planned marketing activities to scream this story as loud as we were able, from coast to coast. We could only hope that our competitors were listening to the consultants' advice. If so, we would start the race at least three months before anyone else, maybe our head start would be even bigger.

Away we went with a radical idea and rabid teamwork to execute our plan. The result? By taking our chance when it came along, a 5-percent-market-share player obtained top market-share position in TFSAs. We sold TFSAs like snow cones on a hot summer day. INGD was the only major bank in the marketplace, opening accounts like wildfire. Even in January the competition was not ready to start—you could walk into any branch of any bank, and nobody even knew what a TFSA was. Our huge head start was helped by the government's awareness program. Most people don't usually think to thank the tax-man—but this time we sure did.

We could have just waited, of course. That would have reduced the risk. But what we were doing had to be different, and in this case it meant creating our own winning conditions. It wasn't only about reaction, it was just as much about anticipation. We had built a machine that could move swiftly, that presented and/or opened windows wider on opportunity, that was flexible enough to recover and strengthen itself in the case of error.

Our team rallied around this new opportunity. We built the product, enhanced our systems, created our advertising campaign, trained our employees, all in the matter of a few months. Simply put, this was the best option for our business, nothing less. One could say we took a risk, but we thought of it as an investment. We'll keep those new clients for years because we were able to prove and not just say that when we win, they win, and when they win, we win.

It's better to get the market share first and fight to keep it than to wage open warfare after your competitors already have a stake. We know this well because we are the scrappy challenger in the market-place fighting for every customer, every dollar.

Love the haters

One day a French-speaking client went onto the French-language section of our Web site and the first tab he got was the English "I'm a Client, let me in!", which is standard for our sign-in page. Admittedly, it should have been in French.

Our technology team had made an overnight change and a mistake happened. The client was very upset and he vehemently let me know. I responded to his email within 30 minutes and told him I was very sorry. His email response was, *I'm fucking leaving.* I apologized again and took some time to explain the problem and how we had fixed it. Why? Because I viewed his dissatisfaction as an opportunity to turn a good customer into a great one by telling him honestly that we'd screwed up. Confessing our errors makes us human, vulnerable and accountable.

A brand is, first and foremost, what people think and say about you. They'll make their judgments based on their interactions with you. They base their views on your marketing, their first interactions with you, their last interactions with you, their worst interactions with you or how you handled a problem. Which gives rise to the question, How does something imperfect improve brand value? In two seemingly opposite ways.

First, if something isn't perfect then technically it under-delivers. It becomes the opposite of exceeding expectations; this is true of a service, a product, or a personal interaction. If people have an expectation of our brand and we disappoint them, whether it's because of pricing or service, or because the process wasn't easy or it was confusing, or it just doesn't work (say you deposit a cheque, and the money doesn't get put it your account)—that damages the brand. But here's the other way of looking at imperfection: if you screw something up, admit the mistake and fix it. This can be even more powerful than getting it right the first time.

In any service industry people are so used to things going wrong and the disappointing way they're responded to afterwards. They're conditioned to expect the worst because that's often what they get.

Of course we make mistakes too. And our customers absolutely point them out to us and not always in a very nice way. But our customer-facing employees and leaders admit our errors and they are able to repair them for the customer with empathy and urgency. I personally get involved here, responding to calls, emails and social media communications. I have observed that an angry customer can become one of your best ambassadors based upon how you resolve their problem. If they come to understand that you listen, that you care and that until their problem is repaired they are all that matters to you, they will love you and tell the story to their friends and family.

In my personal life, some of the closest relationships I have are with people I went to see after pissing them off and asking for a private word. *What is it this time?* they might ask. *I want to apologize. I made a mistake. I'm just really sorry,* I'll say. Admit your mistakes and people will love you more. They'll defend you. And when other haters take action and attack you, you won't even have to defend yourself. The people who love and understand you will jump to your defence. Yes, even your customers.

By the way, the frustrated French-speaking client didn't leave after all. And I'll bet he's told at least five people how we fixed the problem.

So we love the haters. Thanks to them, our army of lovers grows.

Fire customers

When leading change, keep what is best about your culture and rotate around your strengths. —@PeterAceto, January 24, 2014, Tweet

Tangerine is not for everybody. One day we could be. One day, we could be the number one bank in Canada. As of 2014 we were indeed the number one direct bank in Canada, but that doesn't mean a lot because there's very little competition—particularly in direct banking.

By 2020, I believe we'll be the top everyday bank in Canada, which means that we'll have the most customers choosing us as their primary day-to-day bank. We will help them buy a home, finance a car, run their daily lives and save for the short, medium and long term. We will help them to simplify their lives and be happier because they are in control and because their healthy financial habits will let them be worry free.

Companies like to talk about how big they are. Size matters, but it must not be the focal point. We care more about the way Canadians think about us, the influence that we have, the number of customers who have chosen us. We don't want to be a giant commercial bank. We're a retail bank, here for the average Canadian. Bankers often talk about asset size, balance sheets, market cap. We want big impact. We want lots of loyal, financially fit, happy customers. We're here for people's lives. For the big decisions. For individuals building their own future.

To do this we need to be disciplined. Disciplined about the customers we let in, and more importantly about the ones we don't let in. In my early days as CEO, I got wind that a customer had badly mistreated one of our employees by email. I insisted that the account be shut down, which created a shock inside the organization. Since that day, we have proactively closed people's accounts regularly. I have no problem doing that; it's unfortunate, but sometimes you have to cut your losses. Some people who come into our Cafés demand paper receipts for their deposits. We explain that they don't need paper receipts because they can instantly view their transactions online. If the person complains and complains and complains, it means we've captured the wrong customer.

I've often had to explain to customers that we probably won't be able to keep them happy all the time. It's critical for our model that we spend all of our energy on the customer that's the right fit for us. Some people leave turned off, but not very many. I'm not even sure if we track who walks away or not. Either way, it's not important. The good news is that our active customer segment has grown consistently because we were extremely vigilant about filtering customers from day one.

How can a non-banker apply this kind of thinking in home or work life? As with everything else, I try to keep things simple by asking myself a straightforward question: Does this person make winning easier or harder for me? Admittedly, some people make our lives harder but we keep them around anyway because we've seen the good in them and it's worth fighting for. But that's the long game, and it doesn't apply to everybody, always.

Don't be angry if it's isolating

Many use rules and regulations as excuses not to innovate. But real innovators see them as opportunities. —@PeterAceto, March 7, 2014, Tweet

Someone handed me a business card many years ago, and as minute as this interaction seems, it made a big difference in my way of working and viewing partnerships with outside companies and organizations. The card belonged to an Ottawa man who owned a sporting goods store, but it wasn't his name or information that stood out—it was the drawing on the back of the card. Held right side up, a pencil drawing showed the head of a smiling man. Above was written this caption: *Smile and the world smiles with you . . .*

I noticed, though, a type of ambigram in the way the drawing had been designed. When I took the card and flipped it, the face of the man was transformed into a frowning, angry look. The caption now read: *But grouch and you will grouch alone*. It was a very clever drawing and raised an important question: Who wants to grouch alone?

While I was working in the U.S., the regulators passed a rule called Check 21. It required that when a financial institution received a paper cheque, it must scan it and enter it into the banking system as an image. Although Americans still had their paper cheques, the banks moved them around in image form.

Many years later, this process is still not enabled in Canada. When a person receives a paper cheque and sends it to the bank to be deposited, the bank examines the cheque to ensure it is legitimate, makes a deposit entry in the customer's account, batches all of the cheques received that day and sends them via courier to a central clearing house, where they are processed and hopefully honoured by the bank that the cheque was drawn from. Yes, millions of pieces of paper dancing around in the middle of the night when most of us are sleeping. This is very unfortunate.

What does this mean for customers and for banks? Moving images around the system is far easier and cheaper than processing paper cheques. And, with the popularity of smartphones and the camera quality they now have, it is technically possible for customers to take a picture of a cheque and securely deposit it in their bank. Easy and cheaper for everyone. As long as it can be done securely and safely, this is a no-brainer.

The banking industry calls this process Remote Deposit Capture, or RDC. (Tangerine's version is called "Cheque-in.") We had done some pilot testing with employees and decided to launch RDC. Because of the rules at the time, we were able to print those images and put them in the system so they would clear overnight with the other banks, which they did. I remember discussing this with Charaka Kithulegoda, our CIO, the night we put the printed cheque images in the cheque batch for clearing and then hearing the next day that they were all honoured and cleared. We made the decision that we were going to launch this feature, fully understanding that the rules did not expressly permit it.

The change process can sometimes be long and arduous. Sometimes it needs some help, a catalyst. If there had been backlash from our competitors or refusals to process these items, we were prepared to argue our case to the bitter end. I'd do it myself, get lawyers, whatever. This was a chance to change banking again for the benefit of Canadians and, to be honest, it would be good for other banks once they worked their way through it. I was looking forward to a fight, a cause to rally around.

Our leadership team knew that with modern technology, the typical way people deposit money with us would be online. For years now, a person can put a cheque in an ABM machine or mail it to us. Or, a customer can use a smartphone and take a picture of a cheque in our secure app, and it gets processed through the payment system.

Our systems at Tangerine allow us to receive an image of your cheque and process it without any need for the cheque in its paper form, yet the payment rules require the paper cheque when passing the item between banks. There had been an ongoing complaint that the payment system in this country is not innovative or even open to change. Despite this, we decided to go ahead and build new functionalities anyway. We knew this was going to happen, and it was in line with our philosophy.

We advised the Canadian Payments Association (the CPA oversees Canada's clearing and settlement systems) that we were going ahead with RDC. Their reply was surprising; they said they were also considering a rule change, and they added that they planned to do so quickly.

You would think this is great news, and it really is. One day, Brenda Rideout, our executive responsible for marketing and many other things over the years, informed me that the CPA would indeed change the rule and wanted to be a part of our RDC launch announcement. That way, they could say they too were innovative, that they were working with the system, and that they'd helped change the rules. I remember looking at Brenda and saying, "What? Are you kidding me?" This was the perfect frontier to fight on. I was ready. Tuned and mentally prepared.

Brenda and I had been crusading for more than 15 years to change how players like us could access the payment system in Canada. We had tried to build inroads through government relations, met with finance ministers, flown to Ottawa and sat in front of the right people, written letters and White Papers, and visited the finance department to get our point onto the national agenda. And now, the people who had put sticks in our wheels and held up the process wanted to piggyback on our innovation?

Seeing how I felt, Brenda recommended that I sleep on it and suggested partnering would be the best way to change banking in Canada. What a difference a night made. After cooling off it was obvious that collaborating with the CPA was in *everyone's* best interests—theirs, ours and most importantly our customers'. Our innovation would look even more credible, and with this collaboration it had a better chance to go mainstream more quickly. To fight the system is rewarding personally, but is it really what's in your best interests commercially?

For our business, our customers and our amazing employees, sharing the victory in this way was the right thing to do. A smile for them is a win for me, grouches be damned.

Change the things that are easily changed

To understand the technology your customers are using, you need to use it too. Try, test, experiment. —@PeterAceto, December 9, 2013, Tweet

It was date-night for my wife and me. We were at The Keg—which was lovely—and then the bill came. She used our personal ING Direct card to pay, but the server came back to us with one of those embarrassed frowns, harrumphed and told us the transaction had been refused. The card, apparently, had been restricted. Oops.

We called the 1-800 number on the back of the card to investigate. It's never fun to be told your card has been turned down, but as far as experiments go this one could be a doozy. My wife, Sylvia, took the lead.

She was told that the account had indeed been restricted, but the associate had no idea why. She wanted to tell us more but had no information. She was frustrated too. Then the associate went into solution mode. Once my wife had validated her identity, the restriction was quickly removed. We quickly paid the bill with another card, then headed to an ABM to follow the steps that the associate had outlined for us. Quite the romantic Friday night adventure!

We needed to reset the PIN number at the ABM, which was simple and worked exactly as explained. Our associate was fantastic. She did a great job and saw it through to the end.

Many lessons were learned here to improve the customer experience and to empower the associate to be even more fantastic.

For one reason or another, sometimes the bank will have to restrict a customer's card. This is done for their safety and for the bank's. For example, if we find out that card-skimming has occurred at a particular business and we see that a client's card has recently been used there, we will often restrict that card immediately to ensure theft does not occur. But here's the problem: before our (romantic) adventure, the bank wouldn't tell you that we'd restricted your card. We'd wait for you to call us after your card was declined.

While that might be the right technical protocol, it is not thoughtful from a customer perspective. In fact, it's a definite piss-off. If our bank wants that card to be the one you use every day rather than another bank's card, it has to work 100 percent of the time. You, as a customer, need to trust the card will work.

So we had to make a change. Today, customers are notified by email if their card has been restricted. Over 80 percent will contact the bank within 24 hours of the notification. This means the bank doesn't have to let them down when they're about to buy something. Additionally, call centre associates now have the necessary information to explain why a card has been restricted, which is important to know immediately. Reducing stress and anxiety in these instances is crucial. (This change, like at least 20 others, was the direct result of feedback from my wife. She is fantastic.)

It didn't take a lot of work to implement these changes, but it made a big difference in how customers feel. If you are a baker you can't eat the bread you bake just now and then; you have to eat it every day to know what your customers experience.

In late 2013, we surveyed our customers and asked them what they thought were the top 10 changes they would like to see us make. We have tried to apply this kind of thinking broadly, especially online. For example, the Web site features an icon that tells the customer when the last login occurred, what day and what time. Anyone worried about unauthorized access can also sign up for alerts about all activity related to their accounts (another of my wife's ideas). The customer sets the thresholds for the alerts. If your balance falls below a certain amount, if your daughter buys something over $25, if cash is withdrawn from an ABM, you can ask to be notified. People want to stay close to their hard-earned money.

The reason these initiatives even exist is because of our Operational Excellence team, whose primary job is to listen to complaints and fix problems, both short- and long-term ones. They look at the customer experience but they also look at the process and steps. Their brains are wired to find a way to execute a process in 8 steps rather than 10. That's good for the customer and it's good for us too, because it makes us more efficient. It doesn't eliminate jobs—it gets rid of wasted time.

It's about how people process information: if a negative circuit builds in their brains from past experiences, they tend to fall back on that. We're trying to rewire that circuit so people don't go straight to that way of thinking.

The idea is achingly simple: Change things that are easy to change. Don't let small irritations that frustrate your customers grow into big problems that will lose their loyalty.

Retail is detail.

Hang out with high school teachers

Impulse buying is the Achilles heel of the saver. It happens to the best of us. —@PeterAceto, November 18, 2013, Tweet

I've been told that very, very, very rich people get less and less joy from spending their money. The first luxury condo in Miami, for example, is better than the second one in, say, San Diego. The first convertible is more exciting than the next one, and so on.

Nevertheless, the more people earn the more people want and the more people spend. Therein lies the danger with material things. To make matters worse, people who don't yet have the money yearn for those firsts. As with drugs, though, the first time is probably the best time. Afterwards, it takes more and more to reproduce a fraction of the feeling.

It's in this kind of climate that Tangerine coaches consumers to save their money and focus on non-material gains. This is not ideal, but it certainly makes for an interesting challenge. We know that we are fighting very powerful forces of human nature. The reality is that people should be saving at least 10 percent of their earnings before taxes. Tangerine strongly advocates systematic saving in just that way. Many people find it difficult to make that decision, or even just plain forget to hive off part of their paycheque.

With this in mind, we created the Automatic Savings Program (ASP). You can set it up so whatever amount you like comes off your paycheque automatically and goes into your savings account. You don't have to make that decision every single time you get paid. We all know that with dieting, exercise, saving money, anything we try to establish a routine for, it's always the same thing: I'll start tomorrow. Retirement is so far away for most people, they feel like they can put it off forever. With automated savings, the decision has already been made. You save a little now, and it pays off a lot later.

I am not the first person to advocate for savings, of course. One guy I find fascinating is Simon Sinek. With a background in cultural anthropology, this marketing expert seeks understanding of what motivates human beings, of why we think the way we do. What's more, he speaks in real terms, not in fancy jargon. He has nothing to hide. I enjoyed psychology as an undergrad: I have a fascination with what makes human beings tick. As Sinek points out, there are some things about human nature, how humans are wired, that are destructive. Having an automated savings plan, saving in a systematic way, is one way to get around some of our destructive tendencies.

In his book *The Wealthy Barber*, David Chilton makes an interesting observation about teachers. Teachers tend to spend time with other teachers, they tend to live near teachers, they tend to vacation with teachers, partly because they share the same work schedules. Teachers by nature are fairly frugal, and they have frugal people around them, so they are likely happier as a group because they're not longing for things they don't have.

Not everybody is so lucky. Some unfortunate folks live in lovely posh neighbourhoods. This is quite nice, until they realize what's around them: a neighbour with a better house and a nicer pool, another one with a wicked sports car, and another fellow who has three gardeners tending his petunias. It's no wonder some of us spend our lives wondering why we don't have what *they* have. We feel inadequate, so we start spending to feel better about ourselves. Or worse, we borrow so we can spend.

Various pulls and pressures make us feel that we should be spending more. It is in most of our natures to want more, especially when we're surrounded by it. Our daily impulses for a piece of cake, new shoes, or a cool ball cap feel more urgent than retiring in 10 or 20 years.

There are other ways of looking at wealth, and at Tangerine we try to showcase them as much as possible. We once produced an ad campaign in which we featured a company that builds a car out of coffee cups. The message was, again, simple: If you don't spend five dollars twice a day at Starbucks, think of the other things you could have. By resisting luxury, or at least being mindful about how much you spend on non-necessities, you can end up with other things that are better for you. It's a long road with lots of bumps, curves and dips, but you get the picture. Even ten dollars a day will help you retire that much earlier.

Emotion and financial literacy are linked in many ways—understanding our feelings and how money affects our emotional lives. How emotions make us do smart things, and make us do not so smart things. Emotions are tied to financial literacy, because our emotions have a lot to do with impulse spending, with keeping up with the Joneses.

These emotional factors are holding us back and keeping us from living a healthy financial lifestyle. We are human, and keeping that in mind is helpful.

By the way, that car made of cups was burnt to the ground by a vandal. Oh well.

Don't sell, inform

An investment in knowledge pays the best interest.
—Benjamin Franklin

The new suit, from the front, looked just perfect. It had the right cut, the proper stitching, and when he wore it with a pressed shirt and a finely knotted tie, he felt like Gary Cooper. When he walked into the tailor's shop to pick up some pants that had been hemmed, Eli, his tailor, almost fainted.

"Where did you get that suit?" Eli asked.

"Why, do you like it?" he proudly responded.

"No, it's atrocious."

He shot Eli an uncomprehending, bewildered look, so Eli grabbed him by the elbow and they marched over to the mirrors. "Turn around," Eli said, "and take a good look at your ass."

"Oh, my goodness!"

The problem with the ass was that it didn't exist in this suit. From the front, he looked like Cooper, but from the back he looked like a set of unevenly cut curtains. It was awful. Eli made him take the pants off, fixed them on the spot free of charge, and said: "If you're going to buy clothes from someone else, fine. Just make sure you don't get ripped off or look like an idiot."

This funny story from a friend has an informative epilogue. He and Eli both laughed at the time, but what's even more important is that, 15 years later, they're still laughing about it. Eli has remained his guy for years. Needless to say, the one who sold that awful asinine suit was dropped from the roster.

A great tailor is honest and will tell you straight when something you try on doesn't fit. And that's why my buddy keeps going to Eli today—because he knows Eli is not just trying to sell something, even though sales is his job.

This kind of thinking applies to all businesses.

Here's an example. ING Direct came out with a mortgage product and called it the Unmortgage. We advocated that our clients pay down their mortgage as fast as they possibly could, which is not in the best short-term financial interests of the bank. But it's in the customer's best financial interest to do it. Our angle was to empower through knowledge—to educate our consumers about the value of paying down a mortgage more quickly.

But if it runs against our money-making objectives, why on earth would we do it? Loyalty.

Finances are a really important part of people's lives, and having a basic understanding of money and how to save it and how to invest and live a healthy financial life is an important, basic skill.

We're the ones who gave you that advice about your mortgage, and even have a system set up to do it. If you believe that we're looking out for you, you will choose us. Again, that relationship built on honesty and respect pays off with loyalty in the end, as long as your angle is bigger than just making it pay off.

Banks are all involved in helping Canadians be more financially literate. I don't think Tangerine is unique in that regard. But instead of speaking about them I'll speak about us.

You can try to educate people objectively, or you can try to get someone to buy your products. We refer to our approach as advocacy; we advocate for our customers to learn how to manage their financial lives. We are about coaching Canadians to do what we think is in their financial benefit, which is sometimes opposed to ours. It turns out we are known for savings, and savings is a really important part of living a healthy financial lifestyle.

It is beneficial. We want people to be more aware, not saddled with a bunch of things they don't need, further complicating a process that stresses them out to begin with.

You win, we win, hence, everybody wins. This is Weology.

Earn your keep

The Chinese Zen master known as Hyakujo worked in the gardens alongside his students until he was well into his eighties. He most enjoyed trimming the plants, cleaning the grounds, and pruning the trees.

But his students did not understand why he still worked so hard. They felt sorry for him. They discussed ways of getting him to quit, but they knew he would never bend.

One day, one of the cleverer pupils had an idea. He thought, *Maybe we should hide his tools and that way the old man won't be able to work.* He liked his plan, and the others did too. The next day, they hid the tools. That same night, the master did not eat. They hid his tools again the following day. That night, again, the master did not eat.

This sad routine went on and on, until one of the students surmised, "Maybe he is angry with us for hiding his tools. Maybe we should put them back."

The following day, the tools went back. The old master found his usual work. That night, he ate a full meal. Afterwards, he sat at the dinner table and instructed his students: "No work, no food."

If you want the machine to work, the people operating it have to accept their role and find happiness in their own work. This understanding applies to all people, in all jobs.

Earn your keep.

Tell people what they're in for

On the first day of practice, before anyone had even stepped onto the court, the coach stood in front of his team and asked each of his players to answer a question: Do you want to win or do you want to have fun?

He was looking for guidance from the young men he was about to lead, a bunch of 15- and 16-year-olds. He wanted them to make a key decision. Winning, he explained, involves harder work, more playing time for some and less for others, and a different sort of commitment. It won't always be fun, and there's a risk that at the end of the season, we won't win a thing. Winning means sacrifice, pain and struggle, with no guarantees. Fun means everybody gets the same playing time, and the score at the end of the game is meaningless. Unanimously, they voted for winning. What happened? They lost the first game of the year but won every game afterwards until the national final, which they lost by a whopping 44 points.

Overall, the group of players grew together, understood teamwork in a way they hadn't before, and learned the hard way about overconfidence. Ultimately, everybody had loads of fun despite the hardship and struggles the team went through. The thing I appreciate most about what the coach did is this: he had a plan to put in place but was flexible enough to alter that plan based on what his players wanted to achieve. We could even say the coach took his design for the machine, understood the needs of the components and built it accordingly. Everyone was therefore on the same page, striving for the same goal.

There were hard days. The most undisciplined player on the team (who also happened to be the most talented) regularly watched his teammates ordered to run wind sprints because of his own lack of commitment. One day, embarrassed that they were being punished for his lack of discipline and focus, he changed.

The least experienced player sat on the bench more than he wanted to, but he understood the choice he had made. One player who couldn't stand the cardiovascular workouts and constant discipline quit the team altogether—which, it turns out, was good for everybody. His bad attitude negatively affected his teammates' effort and performance.

In the immortal words of legendary Duke University coach Mike Krzyzewski: "A basketball team is like the five fingers on your hand. If you can get them all together, you have a fist. That's how I want you to play."

It wasn't easy becoming one of the best teams in the league. It took a lot of wind sprints and a lot of push-ups. But the players came together like a fist, and nothing, not even losing the final, could break them down. And two weeks after the final, in an exhibition game in a worthless tournament, they beat the team that defeated them in the final by about the same score. No one will remember these competitions because they were just teenage boys playing basketball. No one but the 11 kids who finished the season, and who understood that success starts with hard work and collaboration.

Read to your kids

One of my great joys in raising three great kids was story time. Those years have passed now, but some of my best memories took place while reading stories before bed. The one I always enjoyed no matter how many times I was asked to read it is *A Promise Is a Promise*, by Robert Munsch.

As business people, we read a tremendous amount about vision, mission, culture and values. We consume reports and analyses that prove how these are the key ingredients for a high-performing organization. Those four words, in fact, are the foundation upon which Tangerine was built. They embody the type of leader I am, one who focuses on driving the business forward based on principles, not rules, for people to follow. But when we have really needed to step it up, when the competition has gotten tougher and our plans have grown more audacious, we have decided that we needed to abandon our values and principles and move forward.

As I have garnered experience, I have seen how some plans work and others fail. I have witnessed the countless ways in which the world is increasingly complicated. I have seen people change the core of who they are, sometimes within a single day. Their happiness, stress levels, satisfaction and engagement are on a spectrum, one that shifts and changes based on what is (or isn't) happening at work. The fact is that we are influenced by everything else around us—sickness, stress, an unhappy partner, money issues or something as mundane as traffic on the way to work.

But one thing that doesn't change is how most people truly and deeply understand promises. We learn from the earliest age that if someone makes a promise, that promise must be kept. If it is not, people begin to feel a lack of trust. People have a profound and shared understanding of what promises are—values, missions, visions are esoteric to most of us, but a promise *is* a promise.

When Tangerine decided it was time to shift direction, drive forward, broaden our strategy and accelerate the business, I challenged a small group of our strongest leaders to solve a problem. They were asked to re-examine our corporate values and ascertain how well they had served us in the past. I wanted them to assess whether they were the right set of values to allow us to catapult forward with our strategy.

After a few weeks, they came back and told us that the values we had lived for, that had guided years of growth and success, needed to be abandoned. That these values were now limiting our ability to drive our business forward as we needed to, that they were inconsistently interpreted throughout the business. On top of that, they suggested that we no longer have a list of corporate values at all. Instead, they told me, we should live by a simple set of promises to all of the stakeholders we care so much about—our employees, clients, community and shareholders. Let's all make promises to these people, they affirmed, and let's fight like hell to keep them, always.

It took a lot of guts to come to me with that kind of proposition, and some of the people on the team worried about my reaction. But not for long. I was so moved, I was not too far away from shedding a tear right in front of them. What a great idea!

Promises are so simple, so easy to understand, so easy to share with everyone. They embody where you came from and where you need to be. They combine how you want to be within the business and make a commitment you can share with the outside world. You can ask all of your stakeholders to participate by giving them permission to call you out when you don't keep your promises.

When we introduced our new set of promises to our employees and clients, I chose to use a video as the launching platform so that these groups could look me in the eye and see that I was making the promise both personally and on behalf of the entire organization. And here is what I said:

> When we changed our name from ING Direct to Tangerine, I promised you that even though we will always adapt and grow as an organization, everything you love about us, the things that make us a different kind of bank, will never change.
>
> We have always believed that long-term success is about maintaining strong values as a business. And every decision we've needed to make since we first opened for business has been guided by asking ourselves: Is this true to who we are?
>
> While values are important, they can be a bit abstract. So, to help ensure our values always come across in our actions, we wanted to commit to something more—something stronger. And for all of us at Tangerine, there is nothing more powerful and important than making—and keeping—a promise.
>
> So, we have reinvented our values as Promises. What exactly are these Tangerine Promises? Well, to our clients, we're promising that
>
> - We Dare—By challenging and being innovative to provide you with the best customer experience.
>
> - We Care—By working tirelessly for you, whenever and however you need us.
>
> - We Share—By empowering you with the knowledge and tools to take charge of your financial future.

- We Deliver—We will redefine your banking experience and the role that a bank can play in your life.

We make similar promises to our other important stakeholders—our employees, our communities and our shareholders. We're focused on making sure we keep our promises, and we want our customers to hold us to them.

Not long after introducing the new approach, we experienced a situation where we fell short on one of our Promises. Our Contact Centre faced an exceptionally high volume of calls, emails and Web chat sessions. Clients were reaching out to us with questions about our new name and the changes we made to our Web site. We had several new promotions and offers that were driving a lot of questions as well. Clients were experiencing wait times they should never expect from Tangerine. We simply weren't delivering the level of service clients deserve from us.

So I'd like to take this chance to apologize. We didn't deliver, and I wasn't alone in feeling that this was inexcusable.

One of our fantastic leaders in our Contact Centre also shared her thoughts. Emily joined me in the video, saying:

We were flooded with incoming calls and emails, and our Contact Centre was challenged like never before. We weren't able to get to everyone as fast as we wanted, and it really bothered us. We definitely learned from the situation. We challenged ourselves to find innovative solutions so that Contact Centre representatives can respond promptly when calls and emails are at their peak. We've improved our ability to predict when inquiries will spike. And we've hired and trained new staff to help manage high volumes.

James, also a Contact Centre associate, contributed by sharing his experience:

> I personally dealt with a lot of clients who were inconvenienced during this time. We've learned some important lessons and made the changes needed to ensure we can provide clients with the service they deserve.

I concluded the video by saying:

> Ultimately, promises are a matter of trust. And the trust we have earned is too valuable to ever risk. That's why I'm pleased to share our Tangerine Promises with you. I want you to know about them so that you can call us out if we ever miss living up to them again. Thank you for your continued trust and loyalty, which my team and I look forward to deepening in the years ahead.

This was a defining moment in my leadership. I empowered our people and they created magic. If we have as much success in the future as we are dreaming of and if I am asked about how we did it, I can assure you the answer will be "Our Promises."

We Dare. We Care. We Share. We Deliver.

THE HUMANS

Interactions between We and Me create emotion and passion,
which leads to desire. This desire generates a unique energy that
empowers individuals and thrusts them forward. It makes people
want to be better in their relationships. Or it helps foster
change for those who want to grow professionally.
In the best of cases, it achieves both.

The key to this kind of progress is balance.

It's great to get close to your colleagues, but there have to be limits
because the first priority at work isn't to be liked, it's to deliver
results. To win. It's good, also, to harbour ambition, but proper
growth takes time. The reality is that you will have bad days. You
will suffer lapses when you snap at an innocent colleague or aren't
as nice as you should have been, or grow frustrated at another
person's inaction. But you can't have too many lapses if
you want to thrive in the world of Weology.

I am not a psychologist. But at the office sometimes I feel like one, and that's okay.

A colleague stopped me in the hallway early one morning. We were alone in the building's lobby and he asked me about a charity event I'd participated in, the Covenant House Executive Sleep-Out. This event helps raise funds for and awareness of a great place where homeless youth receive proper nutrition, health care and counselling; learn life and job skills; and get off the streets. I joined over 50 executives, and we slept in a parking lot in downtown Toronto on a cold rainy night in November. Cardboard and a sleeping bag.

As an answer to his question, I fell into my automated, rehearsed Covenant House speech, giving it to him the same way I had 30 times over the past few days. But there was something different in his face as I repeated the story, something that wasn't there when I had told others the same tale. I shortened it a bit and when I was done he replied with something unexpected. I'm not sure exactly what he said but it was something like "Wow, it was great that you did that. It is an important issue that I can relate to." At the time his words went right over my head, probably because I had been in the middle of my blah-blah-blah speech and wasn't really there in the moment.

I wished him a great day, as I always do. Then I headed to the men's room, and as I looked in the mirror it hit me. He was trying to tell me something. He was reaching out to me, and I had missed it. For a guy who thinks he is thoughtful and puts We first, I'd misread the situation. I was upset and went looking for him. I couldn't find him right away but I was inspired to compose the following tweet: "Sometimes we are so used to giving our opinion, as senior leaders, that we talk too much."

My mistake had been to think that I'd given him what he wanted— my story. The truth is that he had a story of his own, but I'd not left any room for him to tell it. About a half an hour later I went looking for him again, and this time I asked if there was something he wanted to share with me, and there was.

When he was younger, he'd had terrible difficulties at home with his father. Physical and emotional abuse. He'd had no choice but to pack a bag and leave. He had been homeless, on the streets fending for himself. Eventually his father passed away and he was left with trying to help his mother and siblings with a profoundly difficult financial situation. Understandably, sharing his story was a very emotional moment for him (and for me), and he was much more eloquent than I am in retelling his ordeal. It was the most shocking part of my day, to say the least, and I'm grateful I took the moment to talk.

Approachability and openness are important for leaders. We need to have a mindset that is ready for an exchange and not merely a broadcast of our own ideas. We have to talk the talk and walk the walk if we are sincere about communication. We also emphasize getting to know one another a little bit more than other places, putting a character to a face and a name. But this requires listening as much as sharing.

Many leaders wouldn't realize that someone in that man's situation was trying to find a way to tell them something important, to reveal something personal, while they were busy holding the floor (that's what happened with me, anyway).

This being said, I also had to end the conversation before it went on too long. We both had to get down to the business of the day. Maybe I was letting him off the hook, or I was letting *me* off the hook by ending the conversation before it went further. It was a thought-provoking encounter—but it was time to get to work. Why? There is a chance you will become the "talkable" CEO if you don't cut things off at a certain point: everyone might start using you as a therapist, as a sounding board, as whatever they feel they need at that moment. To be perfectly honest, I like to be that guy. I actually want to help very much.

Yes, it is great to have real attributes of being open and accessible, and not just by reputation. We strive for it and want it to exist in the everyday real world. But we are a business, and there have to be boundaries. For me personally, boundaries are tough, but they have to be respected.

You can let your people know what you stand for, you can let them know who you are, but that's it. There still has to be some distance, a place where people can't have access. Otherwise you won't get anything done. There is a reason you are going to an office and working on the things you do daily. I've worked for people who were terribly disconnected, and I know how it feels to be sidelined by their disinterest. But I have also been the leader who allowed the connection to go too far, too deep, changing the working relationship and clouding judgment. Leaders have got to find the middle ground. Still, I am so glad my colleague chose to confide in me this way. It meant a lot more to me than I even showed.

I once wrote down this oxymoron: "Get close but keep your distance." A real psychologist would probably be mortified by that line. I am no psychologist.

Respect given is respect earned

Instead of trying to put your best face forward, consider putting your real face forward. —@PeterAceto, October 18, 2013, Tweet

I'm no math professor, but there are some equations that are easier to master than most. Here's one formula that has worked for me every single time: the more respect I give away, the more I get in return.

Obviously, the math isn't the hard part here; it's the whole giving-away-respect thing that gets people excited. Many of us hesitate to trust another person automatically (some would say blindly) because we're scared. We're scared others will abuse the trust or betray it for their own ends. This is normal human instinct, but there is another way of looking at it.

Abuse of trust is the ultimate betrayal, but the perpetrator pays the bigger price: once you've figured out what has happened, you're out of his/her life for a long time. The trust that was freely given now must be earned, and the counter starts in the negative numbers. Such a loss is almost impossible to recover from.

The best way I've found of executing this strategy is to be myself in every setting possible—which for many people is counterintuitive. Normally we have a work persona and a private persona. In many ways we are two different people (at least). My personae, however, are very closely aligned, particularly for a CEO, because I believe there's only so long you can wear two different faces. It must be exhausting to divide yourself in two (or three!) all the time, to always be on guard, separating what one or the other persona has done or might do. That I choose to be who I am everywhere just makes things easier; I don't have to worry about it.

Sure, when I go into a boardroom I know how to behave there, and yes, there's a different filter that goes on in that boardroom, one that's more aligned with people's expectations. But my shareholders see what I'm doing in public—on Twitter, on blogs, in my involvement in charities and community programs and sports—and I couldn't hide any of that stuff even if I wanted to. Yet there is nothing to hide because that's who I am.

Why do people feel compelled to act in that dual-personality way in the first place? A lot of it is expectations about how a CEO should behave, how a CEO should dress, what kind of car a CEO should drive, where a CEO's office has to be.

I recall sitting in one of those traditional downtown private clubs, waiting to meet a colleague for a business discussion. The rules were simple: men must wear a tie, electronic devices were completely forbidden, only the newspapers that were provided were allowed, no whispering, no laughing—heck, no briefcase! You get the picture. My host apologized for asking to meet me there because she knew it was not my style. It wasn't her style either, but in her business she needed to be perceived in a certain way. We agreed that being perceived in different ways to accommodate the situation is a skill leaders have to learn to be successful in the corporate world.

But imagine how liberating it would be to be you, always, no matter who's in front of you or where you are. You know that feeling when you get home and you breathe a loud sigh, rip off your uncomfortable clothes and collapse for a moment. What is that? Exhaustion? Relief? This fatigue comes in part from all of the energy needed to keep up a façade. The hard work of being something other than yourself. Imagine if you could be you. *Always*. You wouldn't make that funny sound when you got home anymore, would you?

Staff do need to know who the real person is behind the title of CEO, or any leader for that matter. You're making decisions about people's lives and welfare, decisions that will affect their families. You're making decisions that have an impact on them and their world beyond the workplace, whether you see it that way or not. If you want them to trust you, you need to earn their trust and be yourself with them.

But it is not advantageous to connect too deeply at the individual level. A clear line must be drawn, and the CEO is the one who has to draw it. Why? Because if it is important to get to know one another, it's even more important to know our purpose, our reason for being. We are here to achieve our vision, to work for our customers, to get the job done.

Sometimes it is a privilege to be taken into confidence, as happened with my colleague who was once homeless; but the reason why this happens in the first place is because we work together. We talk, we get things off our chest—and now let's go back to work.

It only sounds complex: we're just talking about being yourself and being honest all the time, with your overall priorities and goals constantly in focus. If you can manage to implement this principle on a daily basis, it becomes the most rewarding way of working and living for yourself, your staff and ultimately your company.

It's good to know what to expect from others, and from yourself too.

The only expectations that matter are yours

In my years working with the bank, I've had the opportunity to visit many countries and learn about different cultures. My visit to India was life altering.

Tangerine has a small team in India who help us with some of our testing and I looked forward to meeting them. To say the Indians in the office were surprised when I showed up in New Delhi for the first time as CEO would be an understatement. I know this because I read their facial expressions. My summary reading at the end of this trip was this: some of these people think I'm nuts, and a few others think I'm a weakling CEO.

It's all about expectations. Some expect the CEO to have a majestic office up on the top floor, with a big door, and if he (because in India CEOs are usually men) isn't up there, there's something odd going on. When they heard that my office in Canada doesn't have a door, or a wall, and that anybody can walk right in and see what's on my desk, it didn't go over that well. They didn't understand. I was told an open-office concept like ours in Toronto wouldn't work there. In fact, I was told a lot of the things we do—like our commitment to transparency, for example—would fail in India.

They didn't understand why I insist on interacting directly with customers, or why I play shinny hockey with my staff, or sleep on the street to help promote issues related to homelessness. This didn't surprise me completely.

So when I saw the shocked expressions on my staff's faces, I just laughed, but I refused to accept it. As CEO, that is one of the things

I can get away with! It wouldn't work for some people, but to me India is the same as any other place in the world. What the people there needed from me was a first-hand experience with a new way of doing things. My thinking was consistent with our brand: if we give it a try and people live the experience, then we can make it work wherever we are.

Treating people equally and breaking down the barriers between them leads to all the things we at Tangerine believe people are capable of—including a nice dose of happiness for everyone involved. The rest, the big office space, the cars, all of it is just a bunch of silly crap.

Even our own employees in Canada sometimes seem puzzled about the way I am, the informality of many of my interactions, the kind of car I drive. Some are disappointed that they don't see me rolling in a Ferrari. Well, a Ferrari might give them comfort, but not me. At first, my Canadian colleagues were surprised to hear that I wanted to spend time talking with customers in our call centre and at the Cafés. I always noticed a few of them sat up a bit straighter in their chairs when I pulled on a headset and took a call. But over time that changed. One employee always insisted on calling me "sir," but eventually everybody laughed when he did. Some just call me Pete, which has never offended me. It's not something I like, but it's never meant to be disrespectful, so why treat it like an insult?

Human beings come in to work with ideas about the way things are supposed to be, so when they arrive at a place like Tangerine, they can be quite surprised at how everything is designed to work. It is somewhat idealistic to have everyone relaxed and treating the CEO like anyone else, and I have found that some people are genuinely nervous to be in the room with the CEO, but that's their problem. Well, okay, it is my problem too.

All we can do is work to change that kind of image-based thinking, but it takes time.

It's upsetting to me that I might intimidate people. While I can be tough and demanding, I never wish to intimidate. Even when I was a kid I never wanted to intimidate anybody. My goal is to be the guy people enjoy working with—tough but fair, passionate and driven. I want to be the guy other people ask to work with. I don't need to be the screamer or intimidator, having everyone around me walking on eggshells in case I'm having a bad day. But my job title intimidates people because of their expectations of what a CEO must be. Our perceptions are deeply embedded in stereotypes, rather than in how things really are.

By and large, stereotypes are based in fact. They are real, though not always. I am trying to smash down the CEO stereotype because in the long run, the current stereotype for a CEO is not good for anyone.

How to be strong is to know
what makes you weak

At the end of my first year as CEO I wanted to put myself on the line, and I was willing to let the employees dictate the company's way forward. This test would measure the mutual trust we'd built up to then—and if I failed my own test, I'd leave.

I sent my staff an email message that was surely shocking to believe. It went something like this: "One year ago a board of directors chose me as your CEO, but you never got to vote for or against me. Leaders are chosen by people, not boards. Today, you will vote on my future." The results, I pointed out, would be binding and I would abide by them. If at least half the people wanted me to leave, I'd go. If they chose to keep me, they'd have to buy in and follow me. People had to choose one option in an anonymous ballot: *Peter should stay* or *Peter should resign*. (Unlike some referendums, I was pleased with the clarity of my question and the possible answers . . . but I digress.)

When the results were counted, over 97 percent of my colleagues wanted me to stay. Seventeen individuals wanted me to resign. Employees were also invited to share any comments or feedback they had for me. The vast majority of the responses were positive. Some people were offended that I had asked the question. A couple even said that I must be totally nuts to put my fate in the hands of employees. But if I'm totally nuts, I shouldn't have this job in the first place.

There were all kinds of reactions.

- "I've never felt more empowered to do my job."

- "Yes, Peter should stay. Though I don't feel it's appropriate for a leader to ask for acceptance from their team."

- "You've brought arrogance to the executive team. You'd make a good politician."

- "I like the direction the company is headed in."

- "The question is not whether your team has confidence in you, it is whether you have confidence in this team."

- "You had me at hello." (My favourite.)

Some of the naysayers were the types who believe that if you're the president and you don't have a big office, there's something the matter with you. I don't even have my own parking spot; I just drive around, find a spot and walk from there, like everyone else. It freaks them out, a president of a corporation who doesn't slide into the expected status.

It is a tricky balance sometimes: you have to lead, but you want to be more personal as a leader—but not so personal that you don't get anything done. Some employees may perceive your vulnerability as weakness. So be it.

I will absolutely repeat this exercise again someday. Because in many ways, vulnerability can make you invincible.

Forgive physical mistakes,
refuse mental ones

*Leaders must connect with their employees, but that connection should
never stop you from being candid about performance.*
—@PeterAceto, January 7, 2014, Tweet

If you can't trust people, then you can't work with them.

If I am working with a new executive, I give him or her all my trust
right away. That's how I start with people. Credentials are important,
experience is vital, getting to know each other will come, but my
starting position is: I would like to begin a relationship as a trusting
one: I trust you, you trust me.

I give everyone my trust and respect for nothing. Let's start off
with a full tank of trust. The trust meter invariably drops as we make
our way through a working relationship: we don't quite meet expectations, we have to make adjustments, whatever. That's why I build in
some buffers to soften the disappointment. But if that meter starts
falling too quickly, my job is to confront you.

Indiana University's famous basketball coach Bobby Knight forgave
physical mistakes but not mental mistakes: mental mistakes, in his opinion, are more the result of choice than are physical errors. Sloppiness, a
bad attitude and laziness drain the tank of trust. There is no buffer for
these poor choices.

Integrity issues will make that meter drop big time, presuming that I'm right and you've made a serious breach. Things like breaking your promises and not living up to your commitments will also drain away that trust. You promised to give me something on Friday, and you didn't. The tank starts to drain. Accountability needs a 1:1 Say-to-Do ratio to really work. If you say it, then do it, as promised.

Losing my trust happens more often than I might like, and maybe it has something to do with me, not just with others. To avoid disappointment it is necessary to give clear instructions and to be very specific about deadlines and their importance. But misunderstandings and misinterpretations are sometimes unavoidable. Leaders need to be flexible and understanding when it comes to honest mistakes—sometimes the dog really does eat the homework. But when I know that everything was clearly laid out yet problems still occur, there is an issue.

Just tell me how you plan to use me

It's crucial to remember that businesses are run by people—people with dreams, aspirations, ideas and expectations.
—@PeterAceto, November 8, 2013, Tweet

As I write these lines, I can count almost 1,000 employees in my care. I have a tremendous amount of influence over whether they're happy or unhappy. If they're not happy, I guarantee that by extension their families aren't happy. If they had a bad day or they're worried about their jobs, if someone treated them like a bag of crap, if they are uncertain about their future, they're going to go home unhappy. Their misery will ruin more than their weekends, it'll eventually get to everyone around them. And how productive can they be? How much can people contribute if they are living constantly with fear and stress?

It's my job to set people up for success. People, by nature, are good and want to contribute to something worthwhile. Leaders have to put their people in situations that will enable them to do that. There's more to it, though. To start, people need to know what's expected of them, how they're doing, and to get coaching to help them do better. I want Tangerine's employees to be clear about what the organization wants to achieve, what they are expected to contribute to that, and how they're doing relative to those goals and expectations.

Growing up in business, the most I could ever ask for was knowing what was expected of me, and how I was doing related to that. That's it. Sounds simple enough, but this is more difficult than it seems. Executing on those expectations is often challenging. People have different capacities and ambitions. Some of my bosses would say to me, "Here's a job description: just do exactly what it says and we're good." They wouldn't encourage me to do more. You might think that would be a good thing, getting very specific instructions and not having to think outside the box, but I knew I could do more, that I could contribute in a broader way.

Many employees feel this way, with their potential begging to be recognized, cultivated and unleashed. Some are content to just do their job description, and that's fine. But some, if they have the capacity and desire, can do more and want to do more—even if they don't know it yet. I worked for a guy who had me pegged as CEO material, but if Arkadi Kuhlmann had told me that early on, I would have laughed.

You have to have your people in for both the job at hand and going beyond it. You have to give them the chance if they show the desire, to move around the company in different capacities. When they have it in them and don't know it, they will respond to a challenge. Such coaching takes some time, some patience, but it pays off in the long run.

If we don't set up our employees to succeed and give them a vision of something beyond the immediate task at hand, they worry. They micromanage, they obsess over pointless details, they become perfectionists. If we don't do right by them, they feel trapped.

Leaders need to be honest with staff. Let's not kid ourselves: every business treats people like objects. Tangerine does too, it's no secret. But you have to tell them why and how you're doing it. Without that big picture, you cause worry. When the big picture is in sight, people will understand that by working through the tasks at hand, they are being set up for success while gathering experiences.

People leave Tangerine, just like any other business. And yes, some even go to our competitors. Often they leave to get that title they wanted: "Mom, guess what, I'm a VP now!" We try to keep in touch, and sometimes we hear back from them later that they got their title but lost their scope of influence. Their new role is very clearly defined, narrow, rigid, hemmed in. They can't broaden their impact or influence outside of their new job description.

People love to have an impact, to see the results of their efforts, to collaborate and watch the outcome. Sure, you're now a VP, but you're on a tiny island, and someone else is running the ferries. Isn't it more fulfilling, more adventurous—heck, isn't it more fun to be on a team that makes wonderful things happen, makes them happen quickly, and helps customers live better lives?

Employees don't work the same job for 25 years anymore and then retire. Most of today's workers don't even want that. They want to learn, but they want to diversify, to be challenged, to use current skills and learn others. Giving people a shot at more responsibility or different tasks is a great way to set people (and a company) up for success.

But understanding what success looks like and how to get there? That starts with a two-way conversation.

Autonomy is profitable

Diversity of thinking is key to great decision making. Get various experiences and viewpoints in the room when it counts.
—@PeterAceto, December 17, 2013, Tweet

Watching the film *Lone Survivor* in early 2014, I wondered if I could ever make it in the army. I'm not sure I've got what it takes.

Lone Survivor is the story of American soldiers in Afghanistan. The premise is simple: soldiers hunting for a bad guy are faced with a dilemma when farmers wander into the middle of their camp. Will they "engage" with these farmers to protect their mission? Or will they sacrifice the mission to respect the rules of engagement and release the farmers (who will no doubt tell the bad guy)? The soldiers don't agree and the leader has to make a call.

The decision is to follow the letter of the law, and the result is a story that doesn't end well for the soldiers. And I wondered, would the army regret the soldiers' decision to opt for the status quo instead of the alternative? Would that agree with their own view of the Greater Good? It's a tough question and I don't have the answer. I'm glad I don't have to face the kinds of decisions that troops everywhere have faced for millennia. I only hope I can learn from their example.

When I tell someone precisely what I want and how to do it, I get precisely the result I anticipated. When I tell someone the broad-stroke vision of what I'm trying to achieve, and I don't tell them how to do it, I find that the output is way better than I envisioned in the first place. Great people tend to deliver beautiful things, more beautiful than I can imagine myself. The parameters are not strict or confining: the fundamental goals of the plan have to be aligned, but there is a lot of room to make suggestions, experiment and grow.

I regularly have these kinds of discussions with my teams, and they regularly come back to me with results better than I originally envisioned.

You have to be flexible enough to recognize a better idea, especially if it is for the good of the company overall. I try to set it up for people like this: Know what we're trying to accomplish, what your job is, what you're responsible for and be responsible for it. If you want someone to do the job well, then you have to let that person do the job. No micromanagement.

Among the core people who report to me, their primary care is for our business. That's what you have to argue for: the business, not yourself. That perspective makes a big difference. If you make it personal, you put yourself above the business. All of these people work real hours. They're dedicated, and they don't need me to push them. I didn't hire them all, but I picked them all. They are in the right position for them and for us right now—they're challengers.

None of them originally set out to be bankers. They're just all a little bit different in their perspective. *Dirty Dozen*–style team building, remember? One thing they do have in common is vision. I need them to feel independent enough to create; I need to encourage lateral thinking and problem solving.

When I became CEO, two of our senior team members were already with the bank in other roles. I picked them because I wanted them to have bigger roles. Our Head of Product and Revenue is a long-time friend, Robert Landry. A guy I went to law school with. He didn't know much about banking when he joined us but he became one of our best. He's responsible for all of our products, he has a reputation as a special person, and he can hang out with our shareholder because they see him as knowledgeable. He dove in at the deep end and swam brilliantly.

That's what I enjoyed when I started at the bank: I didn't have any idea what I was doing, but every day I was learning something new. All of it was new. Everything was a challenge; everything led to something else. I want to impart that spirit to all of our employees.

Some people liken Tangerine to Robin Hood, who took from the rich to give to the poor—he was truly altruistic. I don't want to overstate, because we are a business. We are changing how people think about banking, and our customers enjoy the fruits of our hard work, and at the same time we make a profit.

Don't ever watch the ball going out of bounds

Don't underestimate the power of your competitive nature. Setting your sights on beating a competitor is very motivating for your team.
—@PeterAceto, December 12, 2013, Tweet

When Dennis Johnson joined the Boston Celtics in the early 1980s, he wasn't particularly fast, he didn't look particularly fit, he didn't seem to shoot the ball all that well, and he often seemed to disappear on the basketball court.

DJ, as the radio announcers called him, had completely changed his approach to basketball. In the early years of his career, he was a high-flying dunker who could also shoot from outside, and a player who didn't get along with coaches. Regardless, he won an NBA championship and earned the Most Valuable Player Award, and then he was traded to the Celtics. There, he became a different player, a new person.

DJ became the guy whose job it was to play defence and pass the ball to any of the five Hall of Famers in the green jerseys. He was the silent leader and it worked: the Celtics won two championships during his time in Boston—including one thanks to his lay-up with time running out.

Yet years after he retired, Johnson is still considered one of the most underrated players of all time. My guess is that you've heard of Larry Bird and maybe even Bill Walton, but DJ is not on the tip of your tongue. Nonetheless, Bird has called him the greatest player he ever played with. Players on other teams have said he was among the very best of all time, but he wasn't elected to the Hall of Fame until years after his premature death at age 52 in 2007.

You might say he finally got his due by not being the guy putting up all the points, but instead by being the leader who did everything else to make those around him better. That was his special ability: understanding a powerful force that makes players mesh with the culture of the team, be what the team needs at a given moment, and sacrifice for the better of the team.

When I look at Dennis Johnson and his time with the Celtics, I see a perfect mix of skill and personality meeting the right kind of team culture. This might explain why the Celtics are the greatest NBA organization of all time. It also sheds some light on the way we look to incorporate talent into our team at Tangerine.

In the early years of the bank, we didn't hire bankers. We hired people whose personal values aligned with the values we needed to succeed: solving problems, customer focus, ability to simplify, an appetite for tough work. People who wanted the challenges needed to pave their own road. We have consistently considered these qualities key. They are part of the whole package we are looking for, and being good and being able to simplify are top of the list. We hire, promote and reward against that.

Change is part of our foundation, because we're in a constant form of innovation. That's how we stay ahead of our competitors. We can't wait for and adapt to change—we have to instigate change.

A company is a group of people trying to do something for customers. If you limit yourself to technically strong people whose skill set lies in one area of expertise only, you lose the humanity because everything is focused on one skill and one skill only. You get people who are like silos, operating by themselves in their own world, and at Tangerine silos are a problem that need to be avoided.

Top universities look at academic transcripts but also put a heavy emphasis on finding out what kind of person students are before letting them through their doors. Skill, knowledge, experience, all these are great; but you have to find good people, the right people for you, your culture and your customers.

Technical skills, while important, are probably not even 50 percent of the solution. Understanding people, relating to people, coaching and teaching, figuring out how to put pieces together to solve a problem—there are so many other skills needed that are bigger than knowing how to price a mortgage. At least, that's what Tangerine insists on. How can you have a team if your employees don't understand the concept of team play, the strengths and benefits that come from teamwork?

If you only have subject-matter experts and they are leading the charge, you're in big trouble. I need the detailed-oriented people around me, but they also have to have equal skills in personal relationships.

I think I know the reason why Larry Bird admired Dennis Johnson so much. I remember seeing a poster of Bird, all six feet nine inches of him, diving after a ball, with this caption: "It makes me sick when I see a guy just watching it go out of bounds." DJ was the same kind of guy, a player who got more joy from a great defensive stop, or maybe a fabulous pass, than from scoring the basket himself. A guy who dived after every ball, no matter what.

Sometimes, somehow, average beats better than average

Mediocrity is like cholesterol: There's the good and there's the bad. Everybody's always talking about the bad and forgetting about the good. I think there's a way to focus on the good mediocrity to build a winning team. Let me explain.

With an employee who's in a position of leadership, who would rate a 7 out of 10, who has really strong, defined strengths, I ask myself: *Should we settle for the 7 or try to find the perfect 10?* From my own experience, when I've made the choice to move that 7 to a different role or asked them to leave, more often than not I've ended up with another 7 as the replacement, after six months of interviewing, reinvesting, acclimatizing, training for the new worker. I look back and wonder if it really was worth it. Sometimes it's better to stick with the 7 you know, train that person and improve his or her deficiencies.

I've consciously had 7s and 8s working in our organization and we all know where they rate; and we also know, all of us, that that's good enough. The 7 who finds a way to help and grow, that's important.

Once in a while, my former boss would say to me, "John is a 5 out of 10, but you're never going to find another guy who's as good at the things he does really well. You'll never find someone who'll fight so hard for the management, the employees, the team. So he's a 5 at his job overall, but he's a 10 at specific and valuable parts of that job. Let's find a way to help him compensate for his shortcomings." Initially I'd go home wondering if my boss was insane. I'd picture a giant WHAT? in block letters. What he was proposing was counterintuitive to every business fibre in my body. I also wondered: How is it you ascertain this person is a 5 anyway? How do you establish a number for a person?

To rate someone strong here but weak there, and to throw out their excellent attributes because they are lacking in other areas, sounds like an excuse to me. Why bother making the change in the first place when you can shift, realign, find somewhere to exploit those strengths? It doesn't make any sense, especially when, culturally, the person is a home run.

Basically, it's the boss's job to create the winning conditions for that employee to succeed. You can change people until you find one who's an immediate 7, or you can look at a person who is a great fit but just a 5 and keep him focused on strength areas, and make him an 8 or even a 9. Heck, why not even a 10?

The machine Tangerine has built has the ability to bend and shift—it's easier than fighting against the trends, the expectations, the typical business mindset.

Tangerine takes pride in its corporate culture. When we find people who know the culture, who embrace it, even if those people are a 6 or a 7, we're okay. It makes much more sense for us to work together and find their best place. Learning, accepting and living the culture can take a long time, and that is something invaluable to us. As to how we end up with these situations in the first place, wondering about the 6s and 7s, maybe our hiring isn't good enough, but we're learning.

We could have a great performer who is a bad cultural fit, or an average performer who is a team player and shares our values. Culture and values are the bottom line when hiring at Tangerine: if you don't walk our collective talk, then you just can't work here. We don't roll like that.

There are some people whom I work with who knock over the china when they walk into a room. Being disrespectful is different from being direct, and they operate in a very direct manner. Some of their colleagues may complain, but there are never issues of abusive disrespect. And these bulls get things done (maybe we need less china, or better shelving?).

From a values perspective and behaviour perspective we're clear. We can't sit idly by and let mediocrity creep in and at the same time be wary about perfectionism. So behave well and embrace the culture. We'll enhance the strengths you have, train for others, and you can still fit in here.

I agree in principle with the adage "Hire slowly and fire quickly." I've made both of those mistakes, hired too quickly and fired too slowly, partly because I believe that people want to be great, and given the opportunity they will improve.

There's an easier way to look at it—by breaking everything down into two qualities: being good at your job and being good at fitting into the culture. People who perform well in both will thrive. People who are high performers but don't care about the culture will eventually pollute your workplace. Low performers who get the culture can be trained to grow. And low-performing, culturally incompatible types must be let go with urgency.

To have a truly high-performance culture you need to manage human resources carefully and thoughtfully. Firing people too quickly for performance reasons can do damage to those watching closely. Be sure you've given each person a true chance to succeed. Being too quick on the trigger is wasteful and can cause people to become risk avoiders and keep-your-head-downers. This is the last thing you want as a leader.

All this being said, I look in the mirror and know I need to be a little tougher. The top performers know exactly who the poor performers are, and it kills them to see their leaders allowing poor performance to continue. I am working on achieving a better balance.

What does cholesterol have to do with this? Well, you need it in your life because so much of it is good for you—you just don't always know it.

Make as many mistakes as possible

Don't be so quick to dismiss someone who you perceive has let you down.
There's a 95% chance they meant no harm.
—@PeterAceto, February 24, 2014, Tweet

The worst thing a person can do after making a mistake is to cover it up. This sends every single bad signal imaginable: lack of trust, insecurity, denial, selfishness and more. It's even worse than the actual mistake because it compounds it, gives it a chance to grow larger, maybe grow out of control. Even worse, it might be repeated.

The great football coach Vince Lombardi once said: "You'll make a lot of mistakes in life, but if you learn from every mistake, you really didn't make a mistake." Every one of us has made mistakes. It's one of the ways we learn and get better. In other words, we need people who can make mistakes.

Throughout my career on smaller teams, on bigger teams, whatever the situation has been, I've tried to look at my team and spot the weaknesses, and then tried to replace them. It is over-simplifying but the basics are there: constantly trying to improve the team.

There have been situations that have led the entire executive to agree on keeping one of these "weaker links" because of the way this person fit in despite not being a high-performing leader, or possessing in-depth technical knowledge. This guy has consistently been at the bottom of the evaluation scale on performance, but we've decided not to worry about it. We've agreed to keep a weak person in that role because it's not an important role for us and there are intangibles about this guy that have made him an integral part of the team.

We're constantly upgrading our team. Not necessarily by firing: you can also help people improve, look closer at their skill set, get training, whatever. Make a shift, get them somewhere to exploit their talents to the fullest. Sometimes this strategy works, and sometimes it doesn't. Sometimes it causes a lot of pain, so there's risk involved. We just look for ways they can contribute to the team, the overall goal.

The reality might be that there is a different place where the employee needs to be. He or she is part of the team. We can all work together to find the right solution. It's what we are doing now.

What does the good-guy-but-not-stellar-leader have to offer? On his own, he isn't so hot. So I guess the moral is that it's a good thing he's not on his own.

Buy a pair of jeans

After an employee asked about updating our dress code, I asked our head of HR, Natasha Mascarenhas, to research the topic—look at studies, best practices, etc. We discovered there is a lot of literature musing on this topic. We asked our employees as well.

Our conclusion after all that reading was that there is no empirical data that proves that workplace attire either improves or degrades employee performance or business success. We also concluded that dress flexibility meant a lot to younger employees and so would be important moving forward. A new dress code for Tangerine could better reflect the world around us and would surely differentiate us as an employer in financial services and make another unique statement about banking. (I loved this part of it.)

If all it takes is a pair of jeans on a Tuesday to get the "Thumbs-up Generation" to like working at Tangerine, why not let them wear their darn jeans? In fact, why not surprise the heck out of them and let employees wear whatever clean, presentable clothing they own whenever they want to? Here's an idea: let's let people dress the way they want to dress from Monday through Thursday, and then create a Formal Friday. Why not?

This is the kind of change that takes getting used to, but not that much. It looks like a low-cost, high-yield proposition to me. First, it doesn't cost the company extra money. Second, anyone who wants to wear a suit still can. Maybe this person will feel even more empowered thanks to the suit. That's a good thing. Third, anyone who doesn't want the lapels can wear something they feel good in. Maybe they'll perform better because they feel comfortable and happy. That's another good thing.

Finally, it will be a signal that what matters most is how you do the work, and not what you're wearing while you do the work.

We now have a casual dress code. Presentable is the rule. It's foolish to believe that clothes define the performance. A supportive team, strong leadership, accountability and passion are the keys. Making people comfortable while achieving all their goals is just another step forward for everyone.

Wearing jeans to work is not my thing. Plus, I'm usually representing the bank in public, and a suit is the ideal uniform for this purpose. One of my teachers, Mr. Bidiak, always told us, "Look sharp, feel sharp." I personally believe this to be true. But this is no longer the case for many people. We needed to move along, and I'm glad we did.

Look at people, not age

Leaders need to build scalability in their organization so it has the capacity to seize opportunities. —@PeterAceto, January 15, 2014, Tweet

A lot of my peers are worried about the new generation of the workforce that is coming into the market. Too entitled, too superficial, too restless, too demanding . . . the list goes on.

Like it or not, a new employee from a new generation is going to be cut from different cloth than you were. The key is looking at it as an opportunity, not a drawback. Flexibility and the willingness to have a dialogue are needed, especially if you want to get the best and brightest on your side.

Studies and articles show that, starting in the 2000s, people changed the way they look for work. They've become even more careful about whom they want to work for. They are asking companies to be better engaged socially, environmentally, culturally and in the community; they want less formal places to work; they want more opportunity to move laterally (and up, of course!) inside their companies. Most of all, they want to be paid fairly for interesting, stimulating work that benefits people.

Some folks don't like these new attitudes but I just don't understand what's wrong with them. If I am going to stick by everything I've written in this book, I have to stay open-minded and flexible and above all be willing to do what's best for our business and its stakeholders.

In the information age, where people have unprecedented access to information, ethics are a growing issue in business. There is a shift towards more ethical business practices, but it is still on very limited levels. I don't know that shareholders are ready for a sacrifice in the value of their shares so that the company they're investing in behaves better. But being a good member of the community is increasingly important for the emerging workforce. I see it with my kids and what they are taught at school: a deep responsibility to the community is instilled early on. This is good for the world.

The relationship between leaders and employees is absolutely changing. It is not "profit at any cost" anymore. That push may not be coming from shareholders, but it is coming from other places, especially your workforce. If you want great employees to work for you, if you want the really talented people, you have to face the fact that they have much more power and more bargaining chips than in the past. In some ways it feels like they get to pick and choose. They care about who their leaders are, they care about transparency, and they want to be involved in the community.

Hiring the new generation allows today's business leaders to tap into exactly what young people are thinking and feeling about the world, and most importantly what their needs are, better than any study or analysis could ever hope to. Smart companies will take advantage of this benefit of hiring young workers.

"The year of birth defines a group, not the individual. Age itself doesn't matter." I wrote that in one of my blogs and it rings very true. Shoving people into categories doesn't benefit anyone, and it won't get many "likes" either.

Put people before branding

We see ourselves as the good guys.

With Tangerine's customers and communities, we believe it is our responsibility to give both money and time. The giving program at Tangerine is called "Orange in the Community," and it gives to a bunch of causes, mostly community development projects. Sometimes it's a program with the YMCA; sometimes it's 200 employees getting together and fixing a summer camp, or going to inner-city neighbourhoods in Vancouver and Toronto and revitalizing an urban park.

But we differentiate between giving and sponsoring. There's just plain giving, which is *I give because I'd like to help you.* And then there's sponsorship, which is *I'll give to your cause, I'll sponsor your team and you'll give me some benefits in return.* Sponsorship occurs when you give money to a group in return for exposure. I've never been quite comfortable with that approach.

Historically, Tangerine's focus has been on giving time and money. Sponsorship would be one way of getting visibility, but historically we've done our marketing through TV and the Web—almost no print—and we do community investment, which is straight giving of money and time.

My thinking about charity has evolved over time, and I am so pleased to see how schools are handling the issue of social responsibility with my children. They understand this so much more deeply than I ever did. For this reason I am extremely optimistic about the future of civilization. In Canada, anyway.

I have come to realize the important role that business and business leaders must play in our communities. Throughout my career I have felt the deep emotional connection of helping people who really need help. Not just by giving money, but by giving time. Connecting with the community. Standing beside the people who need your help. Understanding their difficulties, helping them and actually feeling their gratitude. Building things. Seeing a litter-filled concrete pad turn into a beautiful natural playground in 48 hours. The pride, the tears. It's an incredible feeling of achievement.

Water, cancer, kids' hockey . . . so many companies want to own a single cause, but it's just another media approach to reach potential consumers. Many companies try to connect what they do corporately with their giving activities and somehow leverage the two to build their brand. I'm not sure how that's related to their business. How does it make a difference? Where's the human experience?

When I go to charity dinners and hear the speakers, people are always trying to align their giving with a cause that aligns with their business and brand. I've had trouble seeing how that actually pays off. If you want to own a charitable category (such as clean water) because you want it to benefit your business, maybe you'd be better off just doing more marketing.

Tangerine is a business, we have customers and employees in these communities, and if we are going to make a difference to the community, it's our job to give back. We look at it in two ways: first, it's good for them and good for us; and, second, we need to give to people who need a little bit more help.

Roughly 75 percent of Tangerine's giving budget is directed by our own employees. They pick the causes they care about. If you're not sure about the benefit the business gets from your altruism, why not let your employees direct the giving? You have just as much visibility in the community, and your employees become more interested in giving personal time for a cause of their own choosing. They want to match the financial investment with effort and genuine caring. The last thing they want is for the bank to write a cheque and walk away. They're fiercely proud of what they do and the company they work for. The corporate benefit is twofold: better communities in our cities and proud and empowered employees.

I've changed my philosophy around giving so that I'm personally involved. It's not for my benefit. It's not a branding tool—except for the fact that being perceived as a good member of the community is important. I want people to say, "This is a guy who cares about his community, and he personally gives, and the company he leads is generous and gives of its time and its money. His company looks after their employees, customers and communities."

It's okay to be strategic and have a payoff when you're being good. But for me the bigger payoff comes when a staff member chooses where the giving goes and they are proud to work for us.

Leave room for risky secret missions

Control everyone around you and miss great opportunities.
—@PeterAceto, October 10, 2013, Tweet

As in any business, there are always special missions being driven by a number of people throughout the company. To be perfectly honest, I don't know how many, or what exactly each one is about, and some I don't even know exist. I guess you would call those "covert missions" or "skunk works."

How can that be?

Our senior group of leaders love inventing new challenges for themselves, preparing new missions, and adding them to their existing responsibilities. And better yet, they know when enough is enough and don't need someone (me!) watching over their shoulders.

Our mission-based approach works simply. Often, of course, the missions come from mission control (me again!), and sometimes the missions come from the field—from a manager's own initiative or a colleague's. What is important is that these missions are led by people who understand the needs of the business: i.e., the needs of our customers and what we are all trying to achieve.

The opposite would not work at Tangerine. If mission control were only at my desk, there wouldn't be enough missions. And if mission control doesn't know about the missions right away, that's okay too. Being flexible, being nimble enough to read and react, these are all integral parts of a successful team and integral to empowering that team.

Every branch of our business is aware of our overall goals and what we have to accomplish to reach them. The principles they use for coming up with new projects are not so different from our hiring attributes: problem solving, simplifying and putting the customer first drive our missions.

Look at our technology. Technology is such an important element of how we deliver simplicity to our clients.

We have to be aware of technological innovations, of course, but we use them only as a tool to make things easier. There are lots of amazing inventions out there, but aside from being cool, they are of no use to us: they don't make our process easier because they do not make anything easier for our clients. We're not in the business of cool gadget-making, but of making life simpler and better for our customers.

Same with our products, our marketing, everything: it is all about making life easier. So our projects and missions are always grounded in this reality. We are all aware of these needs, so we act accordingly. It is important that our people have the freedom to innovate.

I don't know how many other businesses are run this way, and I doubt this is the style that's preached in business books. I know exactly why I do it. I've learned from my own experience.

Define everybody's purpose

My friend Lynda played professional basketball in four European countries. She represented her country, Ireland, at numerous international competitions. A natural outside shooter, she was the kind of player who would smile sweetly and then tear your heart out with her bare hand. But when she got to play professionally in the German Bundesliga, one month into the season her coach took her out of the starting lineup. What's worse, he didn't tell her why he'd done it. Instantly, she reasoned there was something wrong with her performance.

To make matters worse, Lynda was an imported player, seen as a star by fans and local media, so her concern was how she was being perceived. *What if they don't think I'm doing enough?* The consequence, of course, was an immediate loss of confidence, and there is no better place than sport to understand how feeling good about yourself leads to playing well—and how feeling bad about yourself can lead to poor performance.

This situation went on for weeks. Nonetheless, Lynda was always the first player to be substituted into the game. Sometimes she'd be sent in to replace the starting centre and play "big." Other times she'd be put at point guard to bring up the ball and control her team's offence. And sometimes she just went into her natural position, scorer and playmaker.

Her playing time didn't differ much, and her productivity actually improved, but in her mind, her ego, Lynda struggled with not being a starter. Veteran players discussed it with her, but the coach remained silent until one day, weeks into the season and unable to stand it anymore, Lynda asked for a private meeting. She wanted to know why she wasn't starting anymore, what was wrong with her play.

To say the coach's response surprised Lynda would be an understatement: "You're my smartest player. That's why I'm starting you on the bench."

He went on to explain that Lynda was the only player on the team who could play any position at any time, on offence or defence. Which is why she was the best person to keep on the bench at the start of the game—this way he could identify who was underperforming on any given day and bring in Lynda to replace her after five minutes. This would allow the coach to introduce a new player and a new strategy early on in a game.

And all of a sudden, she felt like a secret weapon, the Swiss Army knife of basketball (with an adorable Tallaght accent).

That wasn't even the greatest lesson Lynda learned. Just as she was leaving his office, her coach said there was one more thing: "What matters are the players who are on the court for the last five minutes of the game." And then he smiled.

Once her ego accepted that her name wouldn't be heard among those of the other starters, Lynda realized how important she was to the team. Her confidence changed and her play improved, yet none of it had to do with a new shot or a physical tactic. Nobody else needed to know, not even her teammates—that would have undermined *their* confidence.

Lynda's self-doubt was all in her head, or heart actually, because it was emotion-based thinking. Lynda needed to know what her role was, and what was expected of her because it gave her a challenge to meet. High performers need this kind of motivation and understanding.

Essentially, the team got better because two people had an honest conversation about expectations and strategy. It's easy to ask why Lynda's role wasn't made clear from the get-go, but like most things it was a work in progress. It needed time and recognition on both sides.

The whole world could operate on people-first principles like those we have at Tangerine. Everything I've talked about up to now, all the ideas, the philosophies, the things the bank has done, the things we are doing and want to do, all of it is just a blueprint for working efficiently. We chose the fuel for the machine; we chose to make the machine itself out of people.

Why couldn't you use this set of values to run your household? Your charity? Your neighbourhood committee? Your sports team? Your space program? Your start-up company? Your restaurant? Your political party? I think you can. There isn't anything so radical in here that it will take years to grasp: the needs of people are first, you have to act honestly, and communication is a two-way street. All the while keeping everything balanced.

I often wonder how different our society would be if we adopted these principles across the board. I'm not saying this is all flawless—far from it—but it is the most human system I know. And it is working—not perfectly, but working nonetheless.

It comes down to believing in people and believing in yourself. It comes down to wanting to change things for the better for everyone, by starting change with yourself. It comes down to a proper perspective on who you are and where you stand in society.

We all see leaders in the news almost daily, in whatever field, dragged down by shady backroom deals, corruption, lies, double lives, addictions, greed and power going to their heads. I'm sure that at some early point every leader wanted to change things for the better; but they lost their way, caught up in image, power, greed.

When you give people an opportunity to lead, to change, and you give them a framework that makes them the good guy, I believe most will rise to the challenge, stimulated and energized. Tell people what they are needed for, why they are needed for it, how you need them to work, and give them room to think and create. I know you'll surprise yourself with the results.

Pride is not always a mortal sin

Straightforward and authentic communication is most effective. It builds trust, forms communities and ultimately breaks down fear.
—@PeterAceto, November 18, 2013, Tweet

Many of today's business leaders inspire me greatly, yet some seem to have lost connection to their own past. If you go back to around a century ago, to the early 1900s, businesses were a really important part of the community: small, medium and big corporations had a local footprint that was critical to their success. Business leaders were advisers, they were coaches for other aspirants, they helped their city, and they were present in the community. They lived among their employees and their customers, in their communities. (Remember the Guinness story?) They were involved. To some extent they had no choice: it's pretty tough to hire the best and brightest of your neighbours if you are treating those neighbours poorly or ignoring them outright.

At some point business lost its way, and consequently leaders lost their connection. Interests have diversified: there are customers, shareholders, the community, all sorts of different elements that are competing for the same time, resources—for everything. And somehow, at the end of the day, shareholder returns became the only thing that mattered. CEO compensation and reward became based on how the share price did and little to nothing else. Some boards and bosses are getting payouts of tens of millions of dollars in a particular year because of the share price alone.

What of goodwill? Goodwill is part of how a company is evaluated by financial types. Historically goodwill stood for the intangibles that couldn't be valued, like reputation, loyalty and employee engagement. Somewhere along the line, the definition of goodwill has changed. I can't pinpoint a specific time, but certainly the shift started with major events such as the Enron scandals. In the 2000s, fresh off a global economic crash, some financial institutions were fined hundreds of millions of dollars for improper behaviour, for not adhering to rules and regulations.

The message to consumers? *We can do whatever we want, as long as we don't get caught. And as long as the share price is doing well, as long as the shareholders are happy with their return, we keep our jobs and truckloads of dough.*

Those days are going, going . . . It's a shift of reality. You can't hide anymore. There are too many media outlets—eventually the truth will come out. Heck, anyone with a smartphone or an Internet connection is an instant global media outlet.

It is more clear to me now than ever: a company and its leaders have a very important role to play in the world and in the communities that they exist within. This can never be ignored or forgotten. Consumers and employees expect companies and leaders to behave better, and they will demonstrate how they feel about your business with action. The best you can get from being involved in the community is having your employees being proud to work for your company. That's why most of Tangerine's giving activities, both financial and of time, are driven by our employees. I think that's unique, that most companies don't do that.

Organizations have to be good members of their communities. Do you want the best evangelists for your brand, people who are enthusiastic about making their communities better? Be good citizens: Your employees will proudly get involved and promote you, in their own way, to their neighbours. And it will tie in with the corporate goals of healthy profits and a strong share price.

I run a business, and the business is really the most important thing that I'm responsible for. But if my employees are proud to be here, and they're proud to work for us, then I can take great pride in that. And add goodwill to top up my bottom line.

Be good, even when nobody's looking

Why not give a wave of thanks or let somebody in on the road today?
Why not? —@PeterAceto, January 28, 2014, Tweet

I found a young man selling T-shirts in the Zocalo, the world's grandest square in the heart of Mexico City, a few years ago. A rebel's masked face on the front of the shirt told me this probably wasn't government-approved paraphernalia. But the back told a different story, one that, whether one agrees with the actions of rebels or not, contains a valuable lesson.

The words come from Bertolt Brecht, the German playwright and thinker:

There are men who struggle for a day, and they are good.
There are others who struggle for a year, and they are better.
There are some who struggle many years, and they are better still.
But there are those who struggle all their lives, and these are the indispensable ones.

While the battles Brecht talked about can't be compared to modern-day marketing or business, there's nothing wrong with garnering inspiration and learning from other people's struggles and wisdom.

Talking the talk is easy: it's the headline you put on your billboard ad. It's what everybody sees and is told is true. But on its own, it's just a bunch of clever headlines. It's just one company talking. Empty promises. Many consumers mistrust advertising because the delivery on those promises often isn't there. They don't listen to marketing very much. People are more interested in the viewpoints of their family and friends.

What actually makes an ad good, what makes it come to life, is proving that the headline is true—that you can deliver on the promise you are making. After the ad, you've got to deliver. The place where an ad comes to life, where the talk becomes the walk, is not on a billboard and it's not on television or on a Web site banner. It's in action, more specifically, the accumulation of consistent action under one great big banner of an idea.

Tangerine promises a forward banking experience. Blow-your-mind service, innovation, simplicity and price. This is who we have always wanted to be. This is the promise we've made in our advertising, and this is what we must deliver during every interaction we have—phone, Web, email, chat, 24/7/52/365.

So if Tangerine wants the public to believe what the ads say, it needs every single gesture it makes, big or small, as proof. To deliver on this promise with consistency requires that our values and culture create the proper environment. Embedding the principles of simplifying, challenging and fighting for what is in the best interest of our customers helps. How we hire and promote is an excellent example. Our performance reviews and performance discussions need to reinforce these simple but focused tenets.

I never said we get it right 100 percent of the time, but we sure try to.

Saving money is the root of happiness

Many people think that money is the root of evil. This is incredibly misconceived. Money is not the problem in our society—greed is.

I wrote that in a blog talking about kids and money and turning kids into savers. Being a father of three, I want my kids to be happy in life and have more options in the future. Who doesn't want that for their kids? Taking that question further: why don't we do a better job of preparing our children for their financial future?

I have touched on corporate greed and how getting detached from their immediate communities made companies lose their focus on the world around them. But we do that as individuals as well, spending beyond our revenues and causing ourselves stress and worry, suffering poor health and depression, simply because we spend too much, and we don't save enough.

We know that having money in reserve (savings!) creates security and leads to more choices in life. It makes you healthier. As a parent I want to provide these things to my kids, but also provide them with a mindset that will enable them to improve themselves for their whole lives.

What words pop into your head when you hear the word *money*? Here are some common ones that pop up when I ask this on Twitter or wherever: *need, want, more, debt, stress, comes and goes, bills, confusing*. I think we've all experienced these in relation to money. How about the word *saving*? Check out the difference: *peace, freedom, fun, retirement, secure, safe*. People get stressed and lost when it comes to money but know that savings can turn the tables. Tangerine wants to help turn those tables, and we want you to help your kids understand this better and earlier.

Kids love learning. Tangerine has done surveys that have demonstrated that many children have a natural curiosity about money, banks, saving, and how it all works. I also mentioned previously that no one is born a banker. Kids are not born with money-sense. By taking the time to educate them now, we can set them up for happiness, security and freedom later.

We see on a daily basis how adults have to learn to undo bad money habits. Personal debt is at an all-time high and growing. Personal bankruptcy figures keep rising. People get desperate and as a result, they and their loved ones become unhappy, almost chronically.

It is this spinoff of the quick-fix culture that is weighing us down: instant gratification, whatever the cost, whatever the consequences. If you can find a way not to live paycheque to paycheque, there's an opportunity for you to be happier because you're less worried. Saving in a systematic way actually can make you happy. Living hand-to-mouth is never fun.

We have an opportunity to change that course by setting up the next generation with the lifelong habit of understanding money and savings. At the bank, we have some tools we use for this, and there are resources in all sorts of places. These kinds of financial approaches are simple to learn, understand and teach.

There's nothing more important than our children's well-being, when it comes down to it. Hey, I don't want to talk to my kids about saving money and finances all the time. I wasn't particularly thrilled about bringing up the topic with them in the first place. But it is necessary, and we can make it fun as well. The important thing is to remember: a bit of education now will pay off richly for their future.

Having money in your savings account may not exactly be the root of *all* happiness, but it sure helps people sleep better at night. And a good night's sleep has been shown to make people happier too.

Talk to your kids about money

Let's protect our children's future by instilling the value of saving.
—@PeterAceto, November 14, 2013, Tweet

We give too much to our children. We do it out of love, I know, but that doesn't mean it's a good thing in the long run. We stop spoon-feeding kids at a certain point, right? So why just keep on giving them everything they want all the time?

Studies show that most parents would rather talk to their kids about drugs and sex than finance, because those are things that parents actually understand. This is a huge concern. When we give, a kid learns how to receive. The problem is that some lessons get lost in giving, key lessons such as appreciation and merit. And let's face it, a milkshake tastes a lot better after a hard workout than after a long movie.

Sometimes I wonder what ever happened to tough love. I know a man born into fabulous wealth and privilege, one of those upbringings. He had it all: servants, luxury, anything he wanted. No one ever said no to him, because he was the scion of power and money, destined to inherit everything. His education was the best that could be offered, and he worked for many years as a high-level civil servant, with broad executive powers. He was wooed into the private sector, which paid him staggering amounts of money to manage things his way. Eventually, when he hit midlife, he divorced his wife of many years and took up with a much younger woman, retired early, and hit the golden road, propped up by his pampered, charmed existence.

But the money started to drain away, slowly and irresponsibly. He and his new wife spent without a shred of conscience, as he had never denied himself anything. There was a currency crash, an asset freeze, all sorts of changes that made him have to look at his finances. Even he couldn't believe what was going out the window, now that his fortune was finite, but he didn't know how to stop. His unhappiness came to a head when he asked his ex to take him back. He admitted he needed to be cared for, and that debt, never even a word he understood, now scared him. She'd grown up without a penny, earned everything that had come her way, and told him that now maybe he'd begin learning something. Oh yeah, she didn't take him back. I wonder whether, had he learned the right lessons as a kid, things might have turned out differently.

After all, we really do give too much to our kids. They seem to get most anything they want, and don't get a sense of value, or cost. It's just *I need this, I need that.* A lot of it is peer pressure too.

Delayed gratification isn't something we push, probably because we naturally want to indulge our children and make them feel better. And probably because they see us acting in the same way. We not only keep up with the Joneses, we have trouble keeping up with ourselves.

My three children certainly have had a different experience than I did when it comes to learning about the value of things. This is why it's most important to have an open discussion with them about money. Straight talk about where money comes from. The catalyst to having the conversation occurs whenever there is a request to spend. Apps on iTunes alone provide my wife and me with three or four opportunities a week to explain the value of money!

I've met people who have lots of riches and lots of stuff, but who don't seem to be happy. I've personally seen people go through it in my family, and every time the experience has made me want to change my ways.

Let the people say it

Here is the text, word-for-word, that a client delivered, in person, to our more than 900 employees.

When I became an ING Direct client, I did so as a single mom with a beautiful 12-year-old son and over $10,000 in credit card debt, a car loan that was more than my car was worth, a line of credit that never seemed to diminish, a mortgage I didn't understand, and mutual funds that I understood even less. I didn't even know where my retirement funds were invested and, to be honest, I didn't have a clue what a mutual fund was. Over the next few months, I learned as much as I could about ING Direct and slowly began to realize that I COULD understand these things, AND be an active participant in my financial well-being. Instead of assuming that I would be in debt for the rest of my life, I actually started to believe that I could be debt free someday.

So I tackled my mortgage first. I spoke with one of your wonderful mortgage associates to clearly understand my options. An ING Direct employee sent me a PowerPoint presentation that explained how paying my mortgage bi-weekly was not the same as selecting the accelerated bi-weekly mortgage payment option. I was shocked at how much interest I could save!

I started to change how I viewed the money I did have. I discovered that I could live without that 10th pair of fabulous black strappy sandals, and that beautiful chunky ring. I started to make mindful purchases, aware that I had a choice—pay down my debt or add another pair of black pants to my closet. Slowly my credit card debt began to drop, and as it did, I understood even more clearly that the choice was mine: debt free or mindless shopping.

I became confident that I could in fact make good, solid financial decisions. So I decided to tackle the one thing that baffled me the most: mutual funds. I contacted the mutual funds team and was referred to Don. Don was, hands down, the most patient man I have ever met. He walked me through everything, and made sure I clearly understood my options. He guided me through the transfer of my funds from that "unknown" place where all my retirement money used to reside. Now I actually get it. I watch my money grow and I feel confident that I can make an informed choice about where to move my money, and how best to invest it. I know that when I retire, I will do so a great deal more comfortably than I could have when all of this was such a mystery.

Eighteen months later, I am still the single mom to a beautiful 13-year-old son, but I am credit card debt free, my line of credit is paid off in full, my car is worth more than the loan I have on it, and I can tell you exactly how much money I have in my RSP. My financial future looks good, and I know, without a doubt, that I wouldn't be in this place if it wasn't for ING Direct.

The client who delivered that great speech and received a standing ovation is Tammy, and—surprise!—she also works at the bank. In fact, her desk is about three metres from my own: Tammy is my assistant.

It doesn't matter who has trouble "getting" finances—anybody can struggle with that because, well, it's complicated. What really matters are the people who do something about it and reach out to the Dons of the world.

Opposing forces can work together

Believe you can and you're halfway there. —Theodore Roosevelt

In preparation for this section I dug deeply into the roots and histories of both capitalism and socialism. I conducted research on the end of the monarchy and the birth of modern government; I read about Cromwell and elections; and I reread all kinds of interesting texts from Marxists and capitalists and economists and—you get the idea.

I was looking for wise words that could, maybe, create a connection between socialism and capitalism. It was a search for a theory that could combine ideas instead of fragment them. Finally, the best and most succinct source of inspiration came from an unexpected place: actor and comedian Tim Allen. "I don't understand why it has to be either socialism or democracy. Why can't we combine things to get the best of each system?"

It doesn't take a Newton to know that the funny guy may be on to something. Allen does indeed pose a great question: What's stopping us from picking and choosing from both capitalism and socialism to create something new?

Think of what a bank does: it creates profit for its shareholders, it promotes individual profit for both employees and clients, it operates in a free market, and it challenges and sometimes helps change existing rules for its benefit. Those are some core capitalist ideas. But there are aspects of what some call socialism now working side by side with those core capitalist ideas. Tangerine practises some things that Adam Smith might frown upon. Taking care of people before profit margins creates a good balance for us. Human capital, in fact, is at least equal to monetary assets. We get involved with the local fabric of life, trying to open communication doors in our communities. Our Cafés benefit us in ways other than providing monetary profit. These don't show up on the balance sheet right away, if at all.

My thinking has evolved over time. I left school feeling that if I worked hard I should be rewarded. I always recall my father resenting all of the taxes he was paying. If you had a great idea or were successful, you should be able to get rich and richer.

But as I moved through life, observing, my views changed significantly. I was shocked by the division of wealth in big U.S. cities. How well off some could be and how destitute others could be. I saw hardworking people struggling. I see this in Canada as well, and it has altered my perspective.

Maybe, if I'm not a psychologist, I'm becoming a bit of a social-capitalist? I think of it this way. In capitalism you are always working for you. In socialism you are always working for them. At Tangerine, you are always working for everything simultaneously: you, us and them.

We and Me.

CONCLUSION: CLICK!

We are all different from one another. Each one of us is motivated by different needs and wants, nurtured by different events that nobody else knows about. It's where the word *individual* comes from.

But the problem isn't with individuals, it's with the mixing of them. People hear things in different ways. They don't always mix well, and nobody is sure why. It has been shown that when one person says a certain thing, often another person hears it completely differently. Which means that, at best, the world is a constantly changing place filled with constantly changing individuals, some of whom want things to stay the same, and others who live to reject the status quo.

Running a business in this chaotic world is a great leadership challenge. This challenge has been exacerbated recently as the world is changing around us faster than ever. This has occurred because of the confluence of two revolutions. First, there has been a radical shift in the way people think, the way we make decisions. People don't trust ads anymore, not like before, and we're wary of big business. Instead, we choose to trust friends, family and unpaid experts and are influenced by their collective real-life experiences. Second, a form of social upheaval has occurred, prompted by the financial crisis that began in 2008.

We don't want promises anymore, we want proof.

Enter technology. We now have tools that make it easy and instantaneous to connect to people everywhere on earth. Warren Buffett was once quoted as saying that it takes a lifetime to build a brand and five minutes to ruin one. That world is gone now; all it takes to ruin a brand is a single click of a mouse. One click and the world changes opinion.

Click.

When you step back and take a good look at these changes, you understand why and how new generations are looking to support and/or work with businesses that give back, with leaders who take a bit less, or better yet do both. They're looking for jobs that don't require overwork and over-commitment. We often hear that the new generation doesn't want to work, but that's just not true. The world is changing because the world is always changing. The new generations are defining the relationship they want to have with the workforce and that's good. Well, it's good for those who embrace the change and move in step with it. Who knows what will become of those who don't?

Leaders need to embrace listening and collaboration rather than their position of power. Often these competencies are not the focus in business school.

Many of the ideas contained in this book, the lessons as you may call them, are not conventional. Most are not taught in any business schools. Admittedly, I don't have a master's in business administration, and I haven't attended an MBA school, but I've worked with hundreds of MBAs and, well, there's not much evidence that many of the lessons contained herein were covered in their programs. Why spend all this money on an MBA and come out quite unprepared for the most crucial part of leadership—understanding people and human nature? It is true—not everything can be taught in a classroom. Some learning needs to be experienced but more can be done in business programs.

One friend who has an MBA went so far as to tell me that the sham of all shams was his Human Resources class. It was the weak link in the program—weak teacher, unprepared or uncaring students—it was the easy credit, an afterthought. This, in his words, is a travesty.

Everything that matters in a business is connected to the management of its people. As it stands, unfortunately, learning to manage and lead people is something managers learn on the job. It's trial by fire. But trust, loyalty and co-operation are not actions you can impose on people. If the boss says, "Do these things right now," you probably can't. How could you? It would be like telling someone to cry, right here right now. These are emotions and are disconnected from imposable action. The only thing leaders can do is to create an environment that allows and encourages these kinds of emotions. A culture that nurtures feeling and lets it grow to the forefront of the business.

For years, business schools have pushed emotions to the background, even though they are a key to success, in life and business. In many ways, they are the key to happiness. Yet so many leaders struggle to even acknowledge the emotional elements of work and life and therefore fail to create an environment where people can thrive.

I feel a certain embarrassment writing this. To say that I live and I work this way, to admit that emotion plays a big part in who I am, as a person and a leader. Why? Because the "numbers people" think *emotion* is a synonym for "too soft." For "too nice." They think that this is the easy work.

Well, too bad. There's nothing easy or soft about it: it's the hard part of the work.

Putting We first and sacrificing the self for the better of the collective breeds success. It's the only way I've seen that builds businesses that are successful for shareholders, employees and clients in the long run.

MBAs are great, truly great, at finding ways of making the system as efficient as possible to maximize productivity, but it often feels like they've left out the human element. They've learned to stretch budgets as far as possible and eliminate all waste. Any company carrying any so-called fat is endangered in today's world. But trimming the fat doesn't make you a good manager, it makes you a butcher. And the best butcher will tell you that steak cooks better when you leave a layer of fat—it gives the rest of the meat more flavour.

At some point, you're stretching the elastic too far. The real problem is that it's not just a new formula, an economic elastic—it's a person. And isn't a person the most complex thing of all?

The odd thing is that business often acts like it has been leaning toward a more human approach for years, but it hasn't followed through. Take an exercise like the Myers-Briggs Type Indicator test that delivers great knowledge about people and their colleagues. I love those exercises and I've been in the room many times when they've been conducted, and I've witnessed how most people really enjoy the process. The exercise itself helps us learn about ourselves and allows us to find key insights about the people around us. But 99 times out of 100, a few weeks go by and the results don't matter anymore. Everything is gone. The goodwill is vanished. They're just letters next to numbers on a page, in a file, in the lost world of data.

It's quite sad because it looks so promising at first. Individuals who have been through the process think they know more about their colleagues and so having a beer with them some time will be easier, but at the end of the day does it change the way we interact on a day-to-day basis? It should, but it seldom ever does. It's like people who watch a great movie and swear they're going to reinvent their lives but forget about it 24 hours after leaving the theatre.

Many senior managers still don't understand the two most important things about a business: the team and the people on the team. People say it, they get it and they use the right words, they understand every ounce of it, but they don't do a thing about it. There's something about them or the system that is forcing them to believe that people are less important.

I've been there, and I've lived the disappointment.

When it was announced in 2011 that ING Direct U.S. was going to be sold, that was the moment that blasted me out of my professional naiveté. I realized that beautiful things can't last very long—because of the financial system and the stock market and the way things work. Unless you can fund something perpetually yourself, it's going to be eaten by the machine. You can imagine how that made me feel, can't you?

INGD U.S. was good for everyone—shareholders, customers and employees—but the system wouldn't let it live forever.

Click!

IDEAS AND CAFFEINE

*The following are selected writings about the principal ideas
I've covered—culture, community, leadership and more. A lot
of the content is derived from my leadership philosophy, created
and inspired by many life experiences. It demonstrates, I hope,
how my thinking has evolved during my years with the bank,
and can stand for any common-sense philosophy of living.
Hopefully, within each line, you'll find an example
of the evolutionary cycle of ideas.*

*These readings are very important to me. And yes, as cheesy as
it sounds, I call these my poems. They're short, which means
that one or two go very well with a nice cup of coffee.*

CULTURE

Creating a culture is difficult, but it may be the most important goal for any organization. Let's make it simple: culture is adhering to a set of principles that guide behaviour and how decisions are made. You have to decide who you want to be and then define your principles accordingly. For example, anybody can be a banker, but what kind of banker are you going to be? That's where culture comes in.

Leaders need to have a clear view of how they want consumers to experience and perceive them. The only way to enable this, to execute it with success and in a replicable, sustainable way, is through culture. Who you are, who you hire, who you promote, and who you fire. How you behave, and act, on the inside, every day. Your culture is key to performance, your brand and sustainable success.

Although we are now guided by our four promises—We Dare, We Care, We Share, and We Deliver—the founding principles of our culture are based on being simplifiers, challengers and good guys. Our employees strive to simplify the lives of our customers by supplying products, processes—everything. We challenge the status quo— inside our business, in the industry in general, and in the way our clients think about banking and their relationship with us. Lastly, we are the good guys. We give back, we treat each other with respect and we advocate on behalf of our clients to help them live happier and financially healthier lives.

Always have a North Star

It may be unconventional to say this, but you don't need to define specific plans for where your life will be in 20 years. Frankly, it's not realistic. What you need is a view, an idea, a vision. A North Star that beckons you. A calling. And what you most certainly must have is the flexibility to live for it, fine-tune it and rewrite it as you go along.

Planning is about the day-to-day commitment you make to yourself and to your teams to forge the vision as you move forward. We may gain perspective when we look backwards, but unless we apply this forward-looking perspective in our everyday thinking and living, it loses its benefit. But that's what most of us do: we spend enormous amounts of time looking back, we analyze and talk about where we have been, because that is what we know for sure. The path ahead is uncertain, unknown, even scary for some. However, after we filter the necessary lessons from the past, we need to step back into the now. We hear it all the time, "Stop living in the past," but it is difficult to separate ourselves cleanly from it.

There is a huge opportunity to change thinking, to shift the focus on what we do today that allows us to move forward and in the right direction. You have to ask the questions of the future: *Where will my business be next week, next month, next year? Where should I go to make sure I'm getting there when it arrives, and before everyone else?* This is where personal and business energy needs to be directed.

Assessing what you do today will help move your personal life and business forward.

Involve me and I will understand

What do customers want? It's a deceptively simple question, but not many of us take the right amount of time to answer it. Customers can have an important role to play in shaping your business, if you let them.

Only customers experiencing what you offer can tell you how well you're doing—or not. The way they feel when they end a call; how they feel about your products, your Web site, your mobile app: these are all significant insights we should consistently seek out. It's been said that unhappy customers are our greatest points of learning, but happy customers have a lot to share with us too, particularly when we involve them in product development.

Nothing fuels innovation more than having customers involved in defining solutions. It's not a stretch at all: they are the ones who use your products on the ground, in real time, however you want to label it. If you can engage current and prospective customers in meaningful dialogue about their challenges, interests and concerns, if you genuinely get to know them, and if you are open and honest and clear about your purpose as a business, you can build a community of trust. They might even, in time, grow to be ambassadors for your brand.

A typical perspective of some leaders is to boost the numbers—a "Show me the money" approach. But look beyond the sale and invest in strengthening relationships and building brand loyalty. What customers really want is to be appreciated, engaged and trusted, and, of course, value for their money.

Customers have the ability to shape your future and create a thriving network on your behalf if you'll empower them. Underestimating the power of word-of-mouth is detrimental to success. Consumers like to talk, share information, complain about issues and even compliment you. Their opportunities and platforms for doing so are increasing rapidly. And there is little customers talk about more than a pleasant surprise when we value them, involve them and celebrate them.

Transformative leadership breaks down the stereotypes of how leaders interact and speak, how accessible we are, and how transparently and authentically we operate. It's a type of leadership that reminds us that we are all human beings, learning from each other, inspiring each other. Frankly, the job of a leader is never to stop learning.

Engaging with customers is everyone's job, not just customer-facing employees. It's the job of directors, VPs and, yes, even CEOs! You'll get a kick out of responding to and engaging with customers directly, even by email or on Twitter—as much as you enjoy meeting them in person. It's a great way to wow people and also to gauge how you're doing outside the walls of the office.

Everything is an opportunity

Millennials are taking over the world! OMG!

Everyone is attempting to understand the needs and wants of Generation Y. Maybe it's driven by a surge of worry from baby boomers becoming seniors, and those of us from Generation X who have to keep up with the unprecedented speed of change.

It is useful to discuss the latest generational difference the business world is experiencing. But should we be worried? Absolutely not! What we shouldn't do is ignore the opportunity it brings. It can be easy to point at conflicts that a generational divide produces. But is it really a divide? Instead of looking at it negatively, see the possibilities of alignment that the new generation can bring.

What makes a good leader? One vital quality is that leaders seek knowledge, learning and experience. They also create an environment of learning and opportunity for others. They are interested in making an impact. Is that age-specific? Absolutely not.

I was quite young when I started my career at the bank. I had various roles along the way, some aligned with my technical skills and competencies, some more of a stretch. On many occasions I hired colleagues older than me, who had more experience than I did, and had stronger subject-matter expertise. With our combined skills, we built high-performing teams, products and functions.

When I became the CEO, I was 39 years old, and similar to any other new role I had assumed, my first objective was to build an inclusive and open environment. Transparency helps acknowledge the age difference while not getting caught up in it. Then you can be open and honest, liberal with sharing information and empathetic to others' feelings. Dwelling on age differences won't get anyone anywhere.

The year of birth defines a group, not the individual. We each bring unique work and life experiences, and it would serve us better to pay attention to the individual and not place judgment on the generation they belong to. Age itself doesn't matter. Instead, strive for continuous learning for yourself and those around you.

Tailor your dress code to fit your workforce

"*W*hy does wearing jeans on Friday make us feel so much better?*"* This question was posted on Tangerine's internal site and elicited a lot of debate.

One of our values requires us to be challengers: to challenge the status quo, to blaze our own path and to avoid conforming. So, to answer to the question above: Most people said they just wanted to feel more comfortable during the day. Of course, not everyone agreed. And the vigorous debate on the issue made it clear that we needed to rethink our dress code. The dialogue presented an opportunity to review old guidelines and understand the impact this change might have on our business performance and our culture.

We researched the topic and found numerous studies. Some suggested that casual clothing results in casual attitudes about work, while others indicated an upswing in engagement. Ultimately, we had to come to a decision that fit our values and culture, and we decided to give our employees the choice. There's a lot to be said for giving people choice. As individuals we live the choices that we make. The trick lies in choosing wisely.

At Tangerine, we believe that we have a strong culture where performance and customer focus are central. We also believe that if employees are more comfortable, they will be happier in the office. With happy and engaged employees, the levels of commitment and performance will improve even further.

We can't challenge only the corporate status quo, but have to challenge our own as well.

Care for everybody

Job applicants are often taken aback when asked in their interview with me, "Who are you?" It's always great to meet people who have a sense of themselves. There simply is no better value than self-awareness. "Hire character, train skill" is a well-articulated and true sentiment by Peter Schutz, former CEO of Porsche.

We are very lucky at Tangerine to have hired some excellent people. Many know who they are as individuals, bringing a level of awareness that removes potential roadblocks to success. People who are more self-actualized, and recognize the strength in change and in their own personal evolution, are a great bet when hiring.

Leaders ought to approach the hiring of people with a view of abundance rather than scarcity. Consider for a moment how decisions are different when they are made coming from a basis of fear (scarcity) versus a basis of trust (abundance). We enter into a working relationship based on some biographical information on a sheet of paper and a great deal of trust. We have a general understanding of the person's professional abilities and the mutual growth we are both hoping to achieve. This relationship is far from a one-way street.

It's crucial to remember that businesses are run by people, people with dreams, aspirations, ideas and expectations. People who, you hope, want to grow and learn more about themselves. So help them do just that, and get to know your people!

It is in the best interest of a business to develop a culture of abundance. Many leaders hold back because they fear that the better their people become, the greater the risk that they will leave the company.

This thinking almost guarantees that your best people will leave. Investing in each other will almost certainly lengthen the relationship, improve the performance of the person and the business, and create loyalty that will last for a lifetime.

What you can't afford is people who resent their jobs, their manager and your business because you haven't spent the time understanding who they are, and because you've refused to acknowledge their potential both inside *and* outside your organization.

Despite all the openness, support and growth opportunities a company has provided, a trusted loyal employee will sometimes still decide to move in a different direction. These former employees are often Tangerine's biggest evangelists. Their commitment stays strong and their loyalty is unwavering. And while they are out there fulfilling dreams and driving better leadership models, perhaps it's in small part because we were not afraid to help them grow.

We all learn from each other. We inspire and are inspired. We take, share, apply and grow. The next time you think of measuring your success, consider counting a different number: the number of great leaders inside and outside your organization that you helped nurture and create!

Be prepared for all kinds of feedback

Everyone in our entire organization has earned "the right to bitch." Within a very short time of the above message going up on our intranet system, many employees mustered the courage to respond. Leaders at the top have to be as real and accessible as anyone—but despite town halls, face-to-face meetings, regular communication and open-office designs, some teammates still find it difficult to voice their concerns, or even to use first names! "Good morning, Mr. Aceto," the odd few still say.

No matter how open our culture may be, water cooler conversations still take place. No matter how hard we try, there are still things about our business that are bothersome and irritate our employees. Annoyance turns into frustration and the next thing you know, your employees are seriously unhappy—and guess who feels it? Your customers.

Straightforward and authentic communication is the most effective way to achieve clarity. Good or bad, deep down we all like to hear things straight. This is the type of communication that builds trust, forms communities and ultimately breaks down fear.

Once the first handful of employees chimed in, more built the courage to share. Team members started helping each other with solutions to newly exposed problems, and senior executives became committed to fixing issues not previously discussed. The action this exercise in bitching engendered was like a snowball building momentum, size and speed.

We may not have solved major business issues by having this bitch session, but now employees know that it is safe to be heard, dialogue is encouraged, and feedback is actionable. And our senior team is reminded of the power that resides in having real conversations, in honesty and open debate.

In encouraging an open airing of complaints, you may be opening Pandora's Box—or maybe just a big old can of worms. The point is the can exists. Open it up, and let the conversations take place. Leaders have to take the initiative: be an active listener and provide safe harbour for your employees' honesty.

Acknowledge negativity at work

The best way to deal with negativity is to acknowledge it exists. Not even the most positive person can be 100 percent positive all the time. Nothing about that is real or helpful. Being human implies we have good and bad days.

Still, no one likes negativity. Not even my wife, who made it clear I was in a foul mood on our way to dinner recently. I am naturally a glass-half-full type of person, but it was that kind of day, until I met our server whose positive energy quickly turned my grumpiness around. He was exceptionally enthusiastic, happy and keen to make our time at the restaurant enjoyable.

Positive energy is powerful. It is arguably one of the most influential qualities you can have. Positive people expect success, good health, happiness and good relationships, and those things tend to show up in their lives, simply because of their attitude.

Positive energy produces positive results and it affects those around you. Negativity can be harmful. In a personal context, it can ruin relationships with friends and loved ones. And in a business context, it can lead to a culture of distrust, impacting productivity, morale and engagement.

It is very easy to engage in gossip—most of us enjoy participating in it—but allowing negativity to flourish starts to erode the culture, slowly and surely. Nothing affects employee morale more than a negative perspective. Its self-reinforcing nature has the potential to spiral a business into the ground.

While some people naturally exude negativity, there is a reason why it happens at the workplace. And no one put it better than comedian and social/emotional learning counsellor Michael Pritchard when he said, "Fear is that little darkroom where negatives are developed."

People gossip, worry and overthink when they can't control outcomes. It is hard to deal with what we don't know—I get it. But the more focus and worry we place on perceived difficulties, the slower we grow. Negativity destroys great ideas.

Why would a star team keep offering bright ideas if, at every opportunity, they are met with negativity? The more that happens, the more uninterested and disengaged we become. Healthy debate and even-handed skepticism are good. They enhance the growth of thriving business cultures. But negativity never does.

The greatest good we can do for ourselves, and our teams, is to be in control of our individual energy. That we can indeed control, and protect! Are you aware of the type of energy you give off? Are you examining the ways in which your energy is generated? Are you self-aware? To paraphrase Harry Truman, are you making difficulties of your opportunities or making opportunities of your difficulties?

Unless stopped, persistent negative energy will spread like a disease. Just as optimism is contagious, so is pessimism. As I recently tweeted: "Be the positive person in the room today. It's catchy like a bad cold but will make everybody's day better."

The three powerful Ps of people

Wendy has been serving food at the Tangerine offices for over a decade. She is not a Tangerine employee, she works for the food services company we hire to manage our restaurant. But Wendy has been making a difference in our lives at Tangerine, every single day. She remembers everyone and has a knack for making you feel great. Many employees line up specifically for her cash register. I'm sure Wendy has her tough days, yet you'd never know. For 13 years, Wendy has brought nothing but kindness, warmth and positivity to our environment.

Then there's Mr. Ganges. Mr. Ganges is a 70-year-old owner-operator of a small dry cleaning shop in Toronto. He is unwell and has a lot to deal with from behind his counter, but he never complains. Every time I drop off or pick up my dry cleaning, Mr. Ganges expresses his gratitude for my business. He wants me to be happy with his work, and I'm certain he would be mortified if I were in any way dissatisfied. He is not curing cancer, but he is just as passionate about cleaning a shirt as he would be if he were. It is obvious that he cares in a deep way about connection, human interaction and servicing his clients.

Similarly, on a recent trip with my family, Janice, the woman who sold us a cup of coffee every morning in the hotel lobby, made a huge difference in our vacation. There was something different about her. She was so engaging, positive, caring. All she did was pour a cup of coffee every morning, but her pleasant and friendly energy impacted our day.

Positivity can be faked, but when coupled with passion and pleasantness it is unmistakably genuine. *Positivity, pleasantness and passion* make people irresistible. You want to be with them, work with them, have them on your team, buy from them, and follow them. Just ask Wendy, Janice and Mr. Ganges.

Some people naturally possess these traits, but can the rest of us learn them? I'd like to think so. If people truly understood the impact the three Ps have on their energy and the energy of those they interact with daily, I believe we would all prioritize these internal changes. We would do something about them.

I've often talked about self-awareness, and that is precisely what I believe these three individuals possess. It doesn't mean they don't struggle or have bad days, but they have learned to rise above them and protect the energy that drives progress forward as opposed to stalling it.

It's often the simplest things that make the biggest impact. It's not even optimism, or a glass half full attitude. That is a narrow point of view. It is more of an appreciation and gratitude for what you are given and a responsibility you take on to do better with what you have, for you and those around you, despite the hard realities you may face.

"You must take personal responsibility," personal development author Jim Rohn said. "You cannot change the circumstances, the seasons, or the wind, but you can change yourself."

So in the spirit of these wonderful individuals who have made and continue to make a difference in my day, I'll leave you with this: Don't be sucked into everyone else's energy. Be the positive person in the room today. You'll bring everyone up.

See your colleagues as teammates

Sport is a common experience in many cultures. Like many around the world, Canadians tend to cheer for our country during the Olympics and other international events. Sport has the ability to unite and enhance communities.

I always loved the game of hockey but I was really a basketball player. It was in university that I began to play hockey, and today I continue to play a fair amount with my family, friends and teammates on our company team. I have coached both of my sons' hockey teams.

We have hundreds of employees who regularly participate in various sporting teams at work. It's a wonderful opportunity to bring people together from across the business, people who share a common love for sports. There is no better investment of my time than when I connect with my colleagues. And it happens in various ways. But the weekly hockey game, in particular, has provided valuable insights and a lot of fun.

These activities break down barriers and remove, for the most part, preconceived notions of the CEO. With all the open communication and curbing of formality we strive for in our workplace, I am still met with the occasional "Mr. Aceto" or "Sir." But on the ice, or in a locker room, it is an entirely different story. For those courageous enough to join our team games, anything preconceived vanishes quickly.

I remember chatting with an employee who wanted to share with me that his family needed to move back to the west coast. He told me how grateful he was for the experience to work with our company and with me. He told me that one of his most memorable moments was the first time we played hockey together, and how when our time on the ice was done I was always the first guy to drop to my knees and pick up all of the pucks. A job no one wants to do. I did it every single week. To prove a point about me. About Tangerine.

What we learn in team sports has a direct impact on business performance. Sports provide a training ground to practise and cultivate leadership abilities: to play with integrity, teach and learn from teammates and create a culture that people want to be a part of. It is an opportunity to inspire others to a common goal, motivate others to perform beyond their limiting beliefs, and fuel passion for something we believe in. This ought to be identical to a day at the office.

"A good coach will make his players see what they can be rather than what they are," said Ara Parseghian, who coached the University of Notre Dame's national championship football team. The same applies to business leaders. We have the responsibility to transform those around us in life and in business by the actions we take.

I love sports, because of the personal benefits and their amazing applicability to business. The lessons learned and fun we have on the ice together have certainly made Tangerine a better place to work and a better place for our customers, and have a lot to do with our success.

To be natural, act naturally

Customer service isn't a strategy. And it certainly is not the sole responsibility of customer-contact employees. At the very core, customer service and the experience a customer gets must be a part of the "why" of an organization, fundamental to its DNA, values and culture. If this principle is followed, it will filter through all areas of the business and through to the customer.

As a customer, have you ever been on the receiving end of a disappointing phone call, email or in-person visit? We all have. So we know the difference between great and terrible customer service. In many ways we are all experts in this area, and this is what businesses have to remind all of their employees of. They must develop the courage to really listen, to empathize, to make exceptions when warranted, and especially to learn. That is what customers remember.

So Tangerine keeps it simple. No scripts. No fancy talk or words people don't understand. Just associates empowered to *genuinely* listen to the needs of the customer and provide simple solutions. This also means simple products, easy access to online and mobile platforms and great design. Those are the elements that create a climate where great experiences can happen.

There are few things customers talk about more than a pleasant surprise. It's a simple thing to do, to acknowledge someone's concern or question and find ways to help. Those are the interactions, whether you're a CEO or not, that build enviable brand loyalty.

Exceptional customer service doesn't need to be complicated. Here are some insights that have helped our bank become truly customer-centric:

- Empower employees and get out of the way. Once you've defined values and aligned employees, distribute power, get out of the way and allow for mistakes to happen.

- Involve the customer. Nothing fuels innovation more than having customers involved in defining solutions. Ask for feedback. Get them involved and adapt your products accordingly.

- Keep things simple. Remove all jargon, complexity and confusion. Customers love experiences filled with ease, great design and efficiency.

- Remember that we are all human beings. People want to be heard. So be real. Listen. Learn. No two customers are alike.

Motion matters most

If you've been climbing the corporate ladder, you might want to stop, or at least re-examine your approach. With a surge in entrepreneurs and independent contractors, it's become evident that the road to growth is no longer linear and leading straight up.

Businesses today are being created at a much faster rate than ever before. Technology has made it easier to innovate and scale rapidly. There's also an increase in confidence among individuals who want, demand and can actually create a new alternative future for themselves. Now the shifts happen laterally as much as vertically.

Moving up one prescribed ladder is the old way of thinking. The days of employees staying with one organization for decades are long gone. Today one might consider staying put for a long time odd or concerning. I mean, who does that anymore? Oh wait—I did. I was the eighth employee at ING Direct Canada when I began. But in all those years, I reinvented myself and the roles that I took multiple times. That is why I'm still here. And that's also why many of our employees have decided to stay. We are built with an entrepreneurial mindset that aligns with our corporate DNA. It allows us to dream big and take risks.

I have always enjoyed variety in my work life. I have a natural entrepreneurial spirit, and I've been fortunate to have been able to apply it in the many roles I took on throughout my career. Critically, I've been able to nurture and refine it as well. All the while under one roof.

While it's important to have specific skills, our employees are constantly encouraged to keep adding to their toolkit and to collect experiences. The many ideas that our employees at all levels come up with for troubleshooting or innovating are inspiring. Some of that troubleshooting ability comes from the opportunities we create for people to move laterally, a move that's become as important as the upwards one.

Mistakes make great lessons

People are often limited by fear. Taking risks, while absolutely crucial, is at the same time absolutely scary. But without the willingness to make mistakes, we will settle for mediocrity. Sure, we might fail, but nothing will allow us to leap forward faster than failure. There is success to be found in failure, and that is called learning.

Entrepreneurs choose a harder path than most. Instilling this mindset in large organizations is far from easy. But the rise of entrepreneurs and a more daring, entrepreneurial spirit in the newer evolving workforce is a trend that's not going away. You have to be pretty clear about how things work today.

With our Orange Culture fuelled by innovation, collaboration and corporate values, we feel these principles drive positive change and make a difference for individuals, communities and the world. This is why we created Network Orange, where independent business people from various industries come to work on their ideas as part of a unique community. By having a set of independent entrepreneurs right in our own backyard, as it were, we've been able to learn, listen to, and be inspired by the many wonderful ideas that some of these very smart people create.

It's never been more exciting to be an entrepreneur or to be accepted as one. There are many more wonderful ideas to be dreamed, created and established by those of us who believe in the possibility of investing in what we love to do. But ultimately, those who are determined to see things through are the ones that will set themselves apart from the rest.

Winners don't think about losing

In movies, sports and business, there is nothing more exciting than to see the little guy taking on the big guy and winning. Such people tap into an energy that no one can see—momentum, the hot hand, whatever it is—but everyone can feel it, and it's electric. Underdogs overcome great odds through passion and determination.

Where does that passion stem from? Could it be about having something to prove?

I had a difficult relationship with my father, which led to having a strong desire to prove myself and to be successful. I became a lawyer in a big downtown firm, worked six to seven days a week, 14 to 15 hours a day, and was not treated particularly well. When I was told that I would not be hired back to continue with the firm, I felt a gigantic sense of disappointment. These experiences stung, but perhaps became a big advantage. Perhaps they led me to push that much harder to create my own path.

Arkadi Kuhlmann, the founder of ING Direct Canada, had a philosophy for hiring the right people. The candidates with the perfect résumés, credentials or schools, while impressive, at times lacked the intangibles he deemed essential. He wanted those with significant disappointments in their lives, with scars, dents and blemishes, who coupled their setbacks with a determination to do better, because he believed that those tough life experiences made them hungry. Perhaps that's what he saw when he decided to take a chance on me years ago. Perhaps he saw my motivation to beat the odds.

It doesn't matter why or how someone becomes an underdog. What matters is that underdogs always have a chance to win—like anyone else. If you think you are going to lose, you will. Winning underdogs never accept losing before the game, no matter the odds.

Adopting an underdog mentality works to Tangerine's advantage, and not just because some of our personnel were recruited with this quality in mind. We automatically feel it on a psychological level, going head-to-head with the Big Five banks in Canada. It makes us move faster, try harder and think smarter. It's powerful and allows us to succeed.

By staying hungry, we've been able to compete with the giants of our industry. They have established businesses with significant resources and vast budgets, 150-plus years of history and oodles of market share. We love the challenge of being the underdog.

We have to maintain the underdog mentality we started out with, even after significant milestones have been passed, a large employee base has expanded, and our market share has grown consistently. We simply can't take our feet off the gas once something great has been achieved. But how do we maintain that electric energy underdogs have?

Yes, we celebrate the wins—we pat ourselves on the back. But then we move on, quickly, as there is so much work still to be done. We stay nimble. We commit to persistent and positive change. We make more ideas a reality. We remind ourselves of our humble beginnings and live them today, every day. We expect team members to challenge our thinking. And we support a corporate culture of urgency.

Underdogs simply try harder, because we have to. Underdogs challenge the conventional wisdom, break the rules, disrupt the status quo and make a dent in society. Underdogs do, in fact, prevail.

Connect your emotions to your brain, not just your heart

Why is it that certain people are successful, and others who seem equally gifted are not? Why are supposedly average and nondescript sports teams able to beat loaded, star-studded favoured teams? Why are certain companies always the first choice for customers?

Some say it is the discipline and desire to make things happen—to consistently deliver excellence through passion. In addition, we need a clear common purpose. Without it, passion can be irrelevant.

This comes to the cultural mindset of an organization. Connected individuals, not companies, are the ones harnessing the power of influence. If you look at the state of the world in the new millennium, we are in an amazing time of change. Technology is altering our digital infrastructure and how we interact with one another; and organizations are challenged to meet the new transparency demands of customers and employees. Much more is expected from businesses today. To lose sight of or discount these strong factors of long-term change is detrimental.

For passion to be most effective, it needs to tap into a belief system, a purpose for why we do what we do, and it has to match the purpose and values of the organizations we are part of. That is what defines engagement. Are your personal values being encouraged? Is your "why" aligned with that of the organization you are part of? This alignment can't be fabricated or trained: either you believe or you don't. Too much of a misalignment will cause conflict, within yourself or within your team, draining valuable energy that no one can afford to waste.

We continuously gauge the level of commitment employees and customers have toward the Tangerine brand. What is the mood of our organization? How are our customers and communities feeling? Do they believe in us? What do they say about us? Even if we don't ask the questions, the answers are there, in the passionate points of view Canadians and our employees have about the company.

We simply can't ignore the human element in business. So whether we can measure passion is neither here nor there. What's important is that we can't dismiss passion, particularly when it is aligned with a cultural mindset. It has a substantial impact on the bottom line. With passion and alignment nearly anything can be achieved in life and in business. Harnessing this energy is difficult but certainly worth pursuing.

Set goals that aren't about money

Daniel Pink's book *Drive: The Surprising Truth About What Motivates Us* challenges the science behind motivation by asking a simple question, "What really drives us to perform?"

For years, business leaders have rewarded performance with money as a means of acknowledging a job well done. To motivate people to work harder, companies dangled the compensation carrot higher, hoping it would encourage their top-tier performers to work more and achieve an even greater level of success. Performance, reward, and the cycle would continue.

Drive has proven to be such a success because the author suggests that the incentive-based performance model may be flawed: Pink's argument is that incentives don't actually motivate, but instead harm performance because they impact judgment and workplace behaviour. These are obviously some very interesting and challenging ideas for twenty-first-century business leaders. If you strip away incentives, what's left to motivate team members?

My path away from this kind of cycle was made very early on, out of the need to do something for people. I made the decision years ago to veer away from a career in law, not because it did not offer enough long-term incentives. It was instead that working for a company no one had heard of—one that had a mission to change a traditional and well-established industry for the better—motivated me more than law and its incentives, because it would give me more of an opportunity to carve out my own path, to do something meaningful, to learn, to help people. It still motivates me in these ways today.

The need to do good to others is a primal motivation in us all. It's just that some people never take the time to consider following it and seeing how it will further motivate them in ways straight financial incentives do not. This insight is becoming more important as the newer generation of workers is motivated more and more by different things. It's up to us to make sure they feel the power to change things for the better rests inside our company walls.

Transparency is a conversation

Tangerine is unlike any other bank. As you've probably noticed we don't even use the word bank in our name. That's because from day one, we knew we could be something different, something better. Since we first opened our doors, our brand has been built on a simple business model that encompasses connection, engagement and word-of-mouth.

No one can argue that social media is putting pressure on businesses to tackle such topics as accessibility and transparency. And we don't all fully comprehend the direct relationship between social media and return on investment (ROI) yet. But social media has the capability to be the ultimate equalizer in commerce. They fundamentally shift power away from businesses and back to consumers.

Transparency drives organizations to act with integrity and to ensure they become more consumer-centric. In order to survive, building that trust between client and business—between you and me—needs to be paramount. Once that's established, companies will be more responsible and focus on driving value for consumers.

In 2007 Tangerine decided to join the social networks, because they can help align our brand of accessibility and transparency. They are where people share thoughts, ideas, complaints, comments, feedback, praise, needs and much more. And we want to stay close to our customers. We want to listen, respond, share, engage and learn. We are learning a lot about the needs of savers, and how our business can actively respond to those needs, by engaging in the conversation rather than simply being a witness to it. All this through social media.

We want our customers to tell us what they think, to share tips and tools with others, and we will do the same with them. If they've just started a new job or bought their first home, or started saving for a big purchase or an exciting retirement, or have any concerns, our social media sites are another place where they can ask, share, engage and inspire others, much like they would with their friends and families.

What is different and most important is that these online conversations are viewed by more people than ever before. This has put power back in the hands of consumers and at the same time created a powerful tool for allowing businesses to listen, to engage and to serve—whether spelled out in 140 characters, or during Facebook conversations or through video content.

Coming together collectively allows us to harness a power that drives value for all. Social media has become a conduit to connect more people, views and perspectives, and are in turn driving change in our society like never before, forcing businesses to get connected and get engaged.

And that is a very good thing.

Embrace inevitability

Research indicates that a CEO's reputation accounts for up to 50 percent of a company's overall reputation. Whether I like it or not, I represent a portion of our bank's brand equity. I also understand the responsibility that is attached to it. What I say and do as the CEO of Tangerine has an impact on our customers and employees.

Think about when word-of-mouth was king and businesses talked with us, not *at* us. Customers dictated the shape of companies. But over time businesses went through a tremendous amount of change, adding layers of separation between leaders, employees and customers. What has become the conventional business approach is no longer suitable. Radical transformation is needed. We should form trust again, engage and be transparent. Simplicity is required.

The founders of the bank took big risks, invested in a radical idea and went on to develop a simple and efficient business model that would make waves, transform the banking experience and stir things up in a positive way for Canadians. We detached ourselves from hierarchies and organizational charts, and we all believed in the simple cause behind our brand, which is above all, customer advocacy.

There is a growing emphasis in the business world today that branding has become one of the most prominent drivers of value. So who owns the brand? For us it is undoubtedly our customers who own and define it.

What's old is now new again: customers own the power once more. But we also know that leadership affects the brand, internally and externally. The CEO may represent a portion of the corporate brand externally, but the real goal is to form trust, be real and be accessible in order to lead employees internally in becoming the company's own brand ambassadors. For us, it's called "Being Orange." Those values come from customers, and those values are our brand. This DNA is shared across Tangerine, helping it deliver the brand promise our customers expect from us.

Cultivating genuine and authentic connections generates immeasurable commitment. This in turn forms a strong corporate culture and shapes the reputation of a business that will outlive any one individual. The most successful leaders are the ones who inspire the next generation of leaders to own their reputation and share in the brand spotlight.

Success is tied to happiness, not money

We had a group of children visit the bank to take part in Take Our Kids to Work Day, an annual national event. They spent the day visiting our Toronto office and got some hands-on experience in how a direct bank works. During the day they were asked a few times, "Do you know what you want to be when you grow up?" Not surprisingly, very few had a clear career goal in mind as they are still learning about the difference between school life and their future work life. For now they can still enjoy the process of discovery.

The next day, I gave a speech to 475 business students at my alma mater, the University of Western Ontario. The speech was about my view that the best predictor of success in work and life is passion. If you pursue endeavours you are passionate about, you will likely succeed. To do this, you need to first know what your passion is so that when the opportunity presents itself, you will be ready.

The most successful people take the time to discover what they love, then build on it to carve out a career path. They are also honest with themselves and can see the benefits of doing what they love to do as opposed to what they, or others, think they should be doing.

So what is the connection between these two days? Even though I am in the business of banking, a major part of my day is working with people and seeing to it that they are passionate and engaged in their positions. In my early days as CEO, I personally interviewed each new employee. Although technical skills and education are important, finding a company that you believe in and a company that you are passionate about is a more important predictor of a new hire's success. Our unified passion ensures that our clients feel some of the magic as we strive to exceed their expectations every day.

Tangerine has been voted one of the Top 100 employers in Canada. We'll always try to make it higher up the list, but in the meantime, we will continue to keep our passion for our business and our customers strong.

TECHNOLOGY

No company can survive without it, and the speed at which the world is changing thanks to our inventions is dazzling. There is an inherent danger, however, with our constant fascination with technology.

What is important in technology is, fundamentally, balance: success depends on it. Balance comes from knowing when to step away from the machines and rely on human power, or when to automate and let the human beings do the thinking work. Banking is a business that is heavily reliant on technology, so balance is probably more critical to it than to most enterprises, certainly other conventional banks. Microchips and wireless routers are our bricks and mortar. It isn't a question of technology or people: both must work in conjunction, and always with the knowledge that we control the machines, never the other way around. This is balance.

Technology can be very alluring and seductive, but unless it improves the customer experience, it's just a gadget, and money management isn't about gadgets, no matter how cool. Equally important is when to turn off and tune out, to paraphrase a famous saying of the 1960s. Getting lost in the wonder world of shiny new toys is of benefit to no one, and obsession means a loss of balance and perspective. Stepping away gives perspective and allows us to use technology as it is supposed to be used: to help us be more efficient. And real efficiency is the result of balance.

Simplicity, always

Complexity is a silent and slow killer of growth. Yet complexity frequently is overlooked—or worse, encouraged, whether officially or subtly. There are industries and businesses that choose to make things more complicated on purpose, to make it harder to compare prices, to force customers to require advice when they don't need it. But complexity weaves problems that accumulate over time and creep into what you do, layer by layer.

What many fail to or do not even try to acknowledge is that a simplification strategy can result in key contributions to the bottom line. We can take it further: if you ask what consumers really want, they will answer "simplicity," guaranteed.

Today's consumer has no tolerance for wasting time, which makes simplicity an absolute necessity and not a nice-to-have for business. That is why technology is driving many of today's solutions to make our lives easier and more efficient. The tools are there for us, so why complicate things?

I'm a Client, let me in! is the first thing our customers see when they access their accounts on the Tangerine Web site and on mobile platforms. Because that is exactly what customers want: they want to get in and start going; they want less red tape, less complexity, fewer steps to get to what they really want. You know the phone calls that lead to five different departments before you get the solution you need (if you ever do)? That's exactly what we *didn't* want at Tangerine, from day one.

We use more conversational type of vocabulary when we talk with customers and we avoid scripts; we operate with more efficiency and decisiveness, and technology helps us provide to fit the pace of modern living. We so much want our business to be efficient and simple that we formed a small team whose sole objective is to help us simplify.

Simplification that meets consumer needs is crucial to the livelihood of all businesses.

Give technology a seat at the head table

A CEO who does not fully appreciate and understand the impact of technology on any business is missing the point of what is remarkably exciting and fascinating about the world we live in today. Quite simply, if a business is not innovating, it will most certainly be left behind. And nothing helps progressive ideas along more than technological innovation.

Technology is changing everything about our preferences and how we live our lives. And it is altering almost everything we know about business. It's fair to say that IT is now embedded in all business decisions. Or at least it should be.

It takes two. Yes, it's a cliché, but there is no simpler truth for what makes the CEO and CIO relationship work. And that is precisely why it works for us at Tangerine.

Charaka Kithulegoda, our chief information officer, and I never have conversations about specific technologies. Despite my natural interest in technology, he will lose me after a few too many acronyms. Our talks always reflect the need to provide value for our customers and employees by making things simpler for them. We ask each other questions: *How can technology help our business grow? Does this innovation make sense for us? Does it represent our values and corporate culture? Does it meet the needs of our customers?* Our talks are far less about the technology itself, no matter how fascinating, and more about the value proposition for our customers.

Charaka will tell you that our focus is not so much on specific technologies. Instead, we often ask ourselves how do we provide value for consumers? How do we meet their needs? How do we keep things simple? We focus on two areas relentlessly: context and simplicity. Because it's not about a transaction, it's about the experience. Whether you're using an app, browsing the Web site or visiting a Café.

Successful CIOs uncover how CEOs think. They are bilingual in the languages of technology and business. They search the latest technology trends to find the ones that both deliver on their company's business strategy and meet the expectations of the corporate culture and its customers. And ultimately they win the trust and support of their CEO and everyone in the business.

There is always a better way

Change is constant. So you have two choices: you can sit and watch your business's transformation happen without you—and guarantee that you'll be left behind—or you can be an active participant.

Innovative businesses are those nimble and courageous enough to drop old strategies and adopt new ones. There's no question that innovation can be a real challenge, but you won't survive without it. If you're not coming up with the next big thing (or many small things), your competitors are, and faster than you can blink. So how do you find the next big thing? You listen. You observe. You try. You fail. You adjust. You try again.

Ideas are everywhere, and you don't have to look any further than your immediate stakeholders: your employees and your customers. Our employees share their ideas in an internal forum. It's open for suggestions about products and processes, and employees vote on which ideas they think are of value. This has been instrumental in fine-tuning new products and services. Customers provide feedback, which is invaluable for finding what is working, and more importantly what isn't, in the real world.

Lately, innovation has become the currency for business success, particularly in the transformative world we live in today. If you're not igniting the innovation spark in your organization, what's the alternative? Do nothing? You know what happens to those businesses.

If there's a magic formula that will produce breakthrough solutions, every employee in your organization should want to find it.

But quite often, businesses get in their own way. Here are a few suggestions for what you can do to cultivate a culture of innovation in your organization.

- Remove the hierarchy obstacle. In other words, foster autonomy. Most of the time, the best ideas come from those closest to customers, and traditionally executives are farthest away. Let others hold the keys to decision making, and allow for cross-functional roles to ensure a well-rounded view of industry and customer needs.

- Let mistakes happen. Be comfortable with the mistakes, because we learn from failure. It helps modify and adjust ideas and reassess objectives realistically. But don't fail too often because you risk losing your confidence. Simplify the strategy as much as possible and make incremental changes.

- Allow time for adoption. Comfort around change doesn't happen overnight. You're going to experience resistance and maybe even backlash, particularly if the innovation involves behaviour change, but human beings do adapt. The key is getting something in front of them and working on it.

- Balance speed and thoughtfulness. Getting something done is good. Getting it done right is better. You shouldn't need 18 months to execute a new strategy, but you do want to be mindful of making hasty decisions. Don't let speed cost you a great idea. Fight for quality, even if it takes time.

Go, be and stay green

A business must play a role much broader than simply delivering strong shareholder value. This may not be a popular view, but it should be.

When a colleague presented a plan on how to make an environmental difference in our business, we gave him the opportunity to do exactly that. During one of our weekly executive meetings, Martin presented his thoughts on how we could be more proactive about sustainability. On the last page of his very interesting and educational presentation, he recommended that we make room for one full-time employee to assume this accountability—and that he would be willing to move from Vancouver and start immediately, which he did!

I like to use the analogy of a bank account—if you see the planet as a savings account, you'll understand that you can only withdraw so much before it starts to hurt your plans for the future. We certainly can't spend more than we save.

It's not an easy task, particularly when you come to realize that sustainability is far more than merely going green. We reduced electricity use in our offices, achieving a 12 percent reduction over the previous year. We stopped selling bottled water, saving 8,000 plastic bottles per year. And we always minimize the use of paper. But is this enough? These, among other changes, are the bare minimum, the most obvious, and perhaps the easiest to implement.

True sustainability requires that we use all resources responsibly, including financial, social and of course environmental resources. This means understanding and embracing our role in moving towards good management of these resources. Our ultimate goal is to run our business completely free from having any negative environmental impacts.

It's clear that for all major change to happen, innovation is required, and perhaps even disruption: the disruption of thinking and beliefs. And while Tangerine has a long way to go, we are proud to be a disruptor in our own way.

In general, society needs to rethink how it can generate maximum results using the smallest amount of resources. As it happens, our direct business model is designed to do just that. Our use of technology combined with our lack of brick-and-mortar branches has propelled us ahead of the sustainability challenges facing traditional businesses. We serve almost 2 million clients with a fraction of the resources a traditional bank would need! Our clients don't carry costs for things they don't need—and neither does the planet.

Our plan is simple. Eliminate, educate and inspire. We won't just reduce but aim to fully eliminate the environmental footprint of everything that happens in and around our offices.

We are reaching out to our clients—as we have with all of our employees—to help educate them on making purchase decisions that contribute to a more sustainable world. We've started to partner with suppliers and businesses that share our values. We remain committed to learning and teaching so we can continue to improve our sustainability performance and contribute in a meaningful way to a thriving planet where people, businesses and the environment all prosper, now and in the future.

Walks do wonders

We live in a world of relentless demand, going from one small thing to another, trying to meet daily obligations. Information comes at unprecedented speed, and we find ourselves juggling multiple activities trying to keep up. We are fully engaged some of the time and partially engaged *most* of the time.

So what happened to downtime?

One CEO has revealed that he runs for three to four hours at a time at least once a week. No iPod, no music, just running. Is this possible? Where can we find the time to do that? Frankly, I think he is full of it. He didn't look to be in very good shape to me.

Technology and the ability to exchange information in a matter of minutes is fascinating, but more importantly it's a necessity. Managing a growing business with many employees, nearly 2 million customers, governance, compliance, a shareholder structure, email and tactical day-to-day requirements takes a lot of time. But when I find the time to disconnect, go for a long run or sit and think, it is a vastly liberating and mind-expanding exercise to think clearly and deeply. These are the moments when my thoughts are refined, complex problems are solved, priorities are clarified, and I have renewed energy and inspiration to get things done.

As human beings, we have an innate instinct to push that much harder when the pressure soars. We are compelled to do more, know more, experience more. While that is admirable, without pause or setting priorities, we very quickly experience burnout. Downtime seems unattainable. It is, however, critical to find it. A big mistake we make is letting email drive our day. We are constantly reacting to tasks set by others. We are splitting our attention and gravitating towards tactical and self-imposed urgencies. And with the surge of multiple mobile devices, it becomes that much more difficult.

By looking at our calendars, we can see and set priorities, and ask ourselves questions that lead to a better balance. Am I spending enough time with the team? Am I actually present in the interactions I am having? Am I allocating time for personal reflection, family, health? If we're not careful, time flies by and we will be disappointed with what has been accomplished. It's not easy, but we have to recognize the significance of personal reflection in attaining balance.

Technology is evolving, and along with it the ways of *staying* connected. Creating opportunities for disconnection is crucial. Personal reflection time is an individual responsibility, and it must be protected. While corporations have a role in identifying and supporting downtime, the answer lies in awareness of your own needs and opportunities to meet them, which has always been the first step in solving any problem.

COMMUNITY

Tangerine's involvement in the community is deep and genuine, and works on an individual and a company level. Why do we bother? As an Internet-based bank, does it matter if we show our faces anywhere near our actual offices? What dividend does this pay out? Every function we have can be done through smartphone, tablet or computer, and the closest contact we need to make is a phone call.

Such thinking is false. Getting involved in the community isn't a choice or a strategy, it's a responsibility. What you take out from a place you must put back in equal amounts—that's what we strive for. We are established in actual communities, surrounded by real people, businesses, schools and everything else. For us to treat these places as nothing more than a convenience is ignorant and selfish, traits often associated with irresponsible business. Responsibility is what it means to be a good citizen. After all, you want your neighbourhood and community to be a great place. Everyone has to pitch in.

Let the people choose!

What label do we put on a company's charity actions? Is it Corporate Social Responsibility (CSR), Philanthropy, Corporate Giving? How many fancy names do we have for simply helping people out?

The trend nowadays is CSR. This has become a strategy used by businesses (more because they "should" do it); however, it is also equally used to enhance their brand, gain market share and build a competitive advantage. This is a strategy, but wouldn't businesses have those things if they were authentically motivated to give?

Don't get me wrong—it's thrilling to see an increasing number of companies adopt ways to enhance the well-being of others. After all, the role of business in society is much more than creating shareholder value. Every business is part of a community we take from, so we must give back.

We've always believed in the importance of accountability, not just to our shareholders, but to our clients, our employees, the public and our regulators. We make sure that everything we do fits with our purpose, which is to help Canadians live better lives. Sure, as a business we need to be profitable, but we also care about the difference we are making for people and in our communities. The motivation to help is part of our DNA and makes it easy for us to be exceptionally responsible.

Reporting publicly on all of the great community work our team has accomplished is very rewarding. People spend more time at work today than ever before, and we want our work to make a positive difference in the world. At Tangerine we allow employees to direct the majority of our giving efforts. The opinions of our employees matter a great deal, and they decide where our resources will be allocated and whom they would like to help with our time and money. People give 100 percent of their energy when they care and much less when they don't.

Most of our employees volunteer their time toward the causes they believe in, and we as an organization back them up. Our management team insists that we get out in our communities, roll up our sleeves and pitch in. We also get our clients involved, in all sorts of ways: through social media, for example, we've been able to get ideas from our customers on other places we could be contributing to.

It means a lot to us to invest our time and financial support in causes that we collectively believe in. For our employees this approach has generated pride, trust, engagement and a sense of fulfillment from work, a set of matching values between them and their employer. Having a stellar and authentic corporate reputation externally and internally is crucial.

Giving, or CSR if we're going to use that term, is not a feel-good public relations goal or marketing strategy. It's not about aligning your brand to the right cause. It is a commitment an organization makes to be responsible members of the community.

Giving is more than money

We can all agree that giving is powerful and extremely reward-ing. Henry Ford once said, "Time and money spent in help-ing men do more for themselves is far better than mere giving."

Is corporate giving about increasing the organization's profile? Or is it about taking accountability for our role and responsibility as a member of society with our skills, technology, expertise and man-power?

Philanthropy can't be a marketing program. I often think about the evolution of business and the separation that has built up over time between big organizations and consumers. Somehow businesses have lost their way. The shift that society is going through is pressur-ing businesses to again be members of our society, and not to exist simply to maximize profit for shareholders at the expense of society. The shareholders are not the only stakeholders being considered any-more.

In addition to giving money, I've believed that it is important to give our time and energy. Accountability is key, and our charitable projects are geared to put accountability first, to ensure we are mak-ing a real difference. We get our hands dirty. This allows us to person-ally meet the people who are at the receiving end of our efforts, to speak to them, learn about their needs and get involved first-hand.

More than 500 orange-clad employees gathered to revitalize the outdoor spaces around an east-end Toronto Community Housing high-rise complex a few months ago. A resident came to greet us. She stood on a giant pile of dirt and mulch we were using to build the playground area for the local children. She shared her story of growing up without feeling any pride in her neighbourhood, but now her children will feel that missing pride. It was a powerful moment that moved each one of us. To contribute to something that helps residents be proud of the places they live, and to help them feel connected to each other and their community, is a humbling experience.

We need more businesses to operate like members of society—to de-emphasize the black tie dinners and the fancy granite and mahogany offices and truly take part in their communities, make a difference, in person. To borrow a line from Bono, big brands and celebrities are like currency, so let's all use this currency effectively.

We hope this consumer-driven shift towards transparency and accountability of corporations persists, that we see more businesses taking responsibility and stepping up to their role in our society.

Know thy neighbours

Think about the entire construct of the role business plays in society. Can business be good for employees, customers, community, the environment, and still deliver returns to shareholders?

We've all witnessed the terrific contributions that big business has made in creating wealth for economies, individuals and governments. People's lives have advanced with the development of new technologies and significant innovation. And a lot of shareholders have enjoyed the benefits of corporate success. But what about the communities in which we live? You know, the local small business, the entrepreneur with a great idea struggling to get his or her business funded and up and running.

It's time to ask this very important question: what is the role of business in society and in the communities in which companies operate? This is not a CSR or PR matter. It is an issue that must take up space in the business model. We aren't there yet, and perhaps I'm being overly optimistic that we can make this happen soon. But you'll agree a shift from profit-first thinking is needed.

It's almost impossible to avoid getting caught up in the fast-paced day-to-day, month-to-month, quarter-to-quarter cadence of our financial markets and commerce in general. Many incentive structures make it difficult for business leaders to shift their focus from profit-only to a more balanced view. But we ask employees, customers and the community at large to contribute to our success, so they are as important a group of stakeholders as our shareholders are.

Tangerine takes an active part of the ecology of the communities where we live and work through our nation-wide Cafés and our Network Orange program, catering to small businesses. Perhaps coffee, healthy living, live music and supporting entrepreneurs are not the most popular tie-ins to a banking brand for shareholders, but they have undoubtedly brought a great deal of value to our business, our brand, and the many people who live and work near these locations.

Nevertheless, we can't be naive about how business works. It's not a charity, and without profit a business can't begin to positively impact society. But we also know that big organizations won't go poor by shifting from profit-driven objectives to investing in the communities in which they operate. Quite the contrary; much can be gained by adapting a well-balanced approach of profit and social impact into the business model.

If you rethink your business model, which you will need to do in time, it is absolutely possible that employees, customers, community and shareholders can be happy all at once. This is the long-term sustainable strategy that future leaders must be determined to fight for. It's time to redefine old standards and drive forward ideas and business models that are truly good for all.

LEADERSHIP

Being a leader in any situation is no easy task, whether on a sports team, planning a social event, taking a trip with friends and family, in a crisis, or as the head of a business. But what does leadership mean, when you strip everything away? There is nothing more written about or commented on in business literature, but very little of all the writing gets at a simple, practical core readers can at once relate to and put into action.

Being a leader is about being honest. That's it. From there you can go off in a million different directions, building trust, judging risk, motivating employees, staying ahead of the curve, addressing environmental concerns . . . but it always is going to come down to honesty. If you are honest with yourself, and you can communicate that honesty inside a framework that relates directly to the values of your business, you can lead.

Charisma has a part, sure, but even then it differs from person to person. Confidence comes from honesty. If we are honest, we can smash stereotypes and live in the present, not some abstract world of image and power filled with empty platitudes of no practical worth to the real world.

Be honest, be true to yourself, live the values of your company, and you can lead.

I recently stood in front of one hundred of our top leaders. I told them that great relationships are built on a foundation of honesty, not harmony. Harmony is the enemy. To have a relationship, to have trust, you must have honesty and candour.

Boldly go forth . . . with thoughtfulness

When thinking about being bold, risk comes to mind. Being bold is having the courage to believe that the uncharted waters you're about to navigate are worth the journey. It's about having the guts to be different, to stand out from the crowd.

We all know that in today's world, business is moving fast. Innovation is all around us and anyone claiming to be a challenger in his or her industry must take a closer look at how to be bold.

You have to ask yourself questions. *Am I willing to do something most wouldn't? Am I prepared to take a chance? Am I comfortable with doing things differently? Being viewed differently? Almost guaranteeing that you will be doubted and criticized?*

It gets tricky when we confuse impulsiveness for boldness. Impulsiveness is never a recipe for success. Being bold doesn't mean risk taking without thinking. A leader can be decisive while still taking the time to make a bold decision. These things are not opposites and not mutually exclusive. Maybe the main question should be, *Am I thoughtful enough to be bold?* It's not the easiest route, but real leaders do not choose the easiest route.

As humans, it's not usually our natural inclination to be bold, particularly when we deal with larger groups of people, when we are managing different people's expectations, like shareholders and employees. It's safer to leave things as they are, easier to set and meet predictable, incremental, conservative goals that are not going to rock the boat. But that approach will eventually lead to stagnation— death for a business. Leaders need to be looking hard for big ideas and giant leaps of progress. They need to have some audacity coupled with trust throughout the organization that they will make good, smart, calculated decisions. They have to come up with innovative ways to separate their companies from the crowd, then prepare to do it all over again, constantly. Being dramatically different is how they "make a dent in the universe," as Steve Jobs put it.

Being bold is not easy. It will be uncomfortable and scary. It requires a balance, though, between the excitement and energy that come with new ideas and the thoughtful, considered process needed to execute that idea successfully.

Look in the mirror. Think about how you make decisions for yourself and for your business. You should constantly challenge yourself, and your teams, to dream bigger, think bigger and make bolder decisions. Mix in a good helping of thoughtfulness and you will see the benefits of big thinking, of being bold.

Show vulnerability to build trust

Every business, no matter how great, is vulnerable to decline. There is something, however, that can protect your business from critical decline: real leadership.

Decline is in the natural ebb and flow of business. It is inevitable and you have to accept the fact that some quarters will be worse than others. So how do you begin to avoid serious decline? What you do is you earn trust. To lead today, you need to be very much "of the people." Leaders need to be relatable, real, fallible—human!

People are too smart to believe that their leaders are perfect, and pretending you are so, or pretending problems do not exist, only insults their intelligence and does your business a disservice. Demonstrating who you really are is fundamental. Your willingness to show vulnerability, emotion and weakness is fundamental to your team. Who you are is of the utmost importance in leading and succeeding.

But what are your intentions? This must be crystal clear. If you undergo a transformation, if you ask your teams to push the envelope and take giant leaps of change, would they do it? Why would they believe you? Why would they follow you?

Leadership is about leading your people, and you can do that only through building trust. Having a vision, inspiring your teams, driving success, taking responsibility for you, for them, for their families and for your customers is what it's all about. Nothing creates trust more than admitting mistakes and revealing weak points: you are relying on others for help.

The buck stops here, as they say, with the CEO. So what is your agenda? Does your CEO title define you? Or are you keeping your ego in check? Leaders must balance power with humility and responsibility. You must put the interest of the business and its people ahead of personal success. If you work for the best interests of your business and your team, you automatically generate personal success for yourself. The moment you make it about yourself, you lose credibility and trust. So avoid any ambiguity about your leadership. Make your intentions clear. Champion your people and your business. Even if you're criticized and even if you're doubted, put your people first. That is what earns trust.

This is what Simon Sinek talks about in his book *Leaders Eat Last: Why Some Teams Pull Together and Others Don't*—a title that can be interpreted literally. Sinek lists the example of the Marine Corps, where men and women are willing to risk their lives for each other. Why? Because they know others would do the same for them. Are you willing to eat last? If you translate this attitude to business, and buy into the Marines' human support mentality, you will stop underestimating your personal capacity for change. When you know your colleagues and especially your leaders will back you up, no matter what, you will be more willing, more motivated and more inspired to take bigger risks.

Do what works for you

B reakfast is the new lunch? This idea is making the rounds in the latest leadership research. Several new articles indicate a connection between early risers and high achievers. It could be true, but more importantly you have to discover what works for you.

Benjamin Franklin claimed, "Early to bed and early to rise makes a man healthy, wealthy and wise." It's nice to believe it's really that easy and can apply to everyone. But a better predictor of success is the highly beneficial but underrated quality of self-awareness. Understanding what works for each of us individually sets the tone for our performance and productivity.

Do you check your phone as soon as you wake up? Do you get to the office, log on and check your email right away? Are you running from one meeting to another, and before you know it you've lost your day entirely? We all do this to some extent, paying the price of living in a super-connected world. At times this leads us to lose sight of our personal connection towards others, and self-awareness for ourselves.

I am lucky in that rising early comes naturally. I am most alert and energetic in the morning. But I've also set priorities that work with my natural rhythm and support both my professional and personal responsibilities. When I arrive early to the office, I spend my time on creative thinking, visualization and reflection. Allocating time to connect with yourself is very important for all leaders: it grounds you, gives you perspective and prioritization. That is how I'm able to set the tone for the day ahead.

I also enjoy what naturally happens early in the mornings at the office: hallway gatherings, one-on-one discussions, and informal coffees. I learn a great deal about our business and who our team members are from those early morning chats. Their hobbies, passions, and what drives them come across easier and faster outside the nine-to-five. Typically I find myself in an unplanned breakfast at least twice a week, always an enjoyable and insightful experience.

Finding those informal pockets in the day to connect with colleagues is valuable for any leader. And it's clear why we are starting to choose breakfast over lunch. What you do before 8 a.m., whether meeting with colleagues or taking the time for reflection, gives you plenty of time to proceed with the business of your day. It allows you to move through your day with less anxiety and a sense of accomplishment.

Maybe the success scale does tip heavier in favour of those wired to rise early. But that sounds silly. There are plenty of success stories about those who prefer to begin their day when the sun is already up. One common thread among successful leaders, regardless of when they wake up, is that they shape a positive and productive workday for themselves and for those around them. By becoming aware of their environment, taking the time to reflect, they define their priorities clearly and manage their time.

While we may lead others, we decisively lead ourselves.

It's not bragging if you can do it

A thletes have a tremendous amount of discipline, training and physicality that carry them through to championships. But what we often underestimate is the level of mental training that it takes for these athletes to achieve their goals. The mental roadblocks they work to remove are ultimately what make some champions stand out from the rest.

It's no different in life or business. How many times have you heard "Choose your thoughts wisely" or "You are what you think" or "Focus on your successes, not your failures"? But have you actually put that advice into practice?

Our thoughts and what we believe about ourselves can either cage or unlock our potential. But they also unlock the potential of our teams in how we lead them. There is an importance we must put on awareness: we must be aware of what runs through our head, both negative and positive, and how we can use our thoughts to drive action, whether for ourselves or for our teams.

Leaders must create an environment where great things can happen. It's easy to fall into a pattern where you spend most of your time focused on what is not going well. Yes, time should be spent on that too, but being consistently focused on the negative leads to a decline in the energy and productivity of our teams and team members. We need to spend more time focused on what is going right, and we must celebrate even our smallest achievements.

Recognition is an often forgotten trait of great leadership. Praise fuels people's energy. Make a habit of applauding the contribution of the individuals who impact the greater success of the team. Don't spend 95 percent of your time telling the people around you what is wrong, or what can be done better. Focus on what they are doing well, find those moments of brilliance in every day, and build off of them until they fill your days and colour the experiences of your customers.

I have already attempted to alter my own behaviour at the office, with my kids and on the ice. I coach my son's hockey team, and we are now spending much more time focused on what the kids do extremely well. At Tangerine, we are prioritizing and requiring our leaders to share recognition—it's as important to our success as the customer experience, hitting the numbers and other priorities.

I've made a few changes personally and professionally, and the benefits are tangible, there for all to see. What will you do to harness the power of your thoughts?

Accept change

Many people believe that change is bad. They typically fear the unknown. But others understand that change creates opportunities. You have to experience change, learn its value and become comfortable with it—even come to love it. Not much is guaranteed in life other than change. Change is constant. So you either manage it, or it manages you.

At Tangerine we've certainly adapted that mentality with a number of innovations and operational changes to meet the times we live in. Change in that sense is in our control. It is essentially part of our DNA. Interestingly, we share a core value with the Occupy Movement, evident when we look at its charter:

> *#10. **We will be heard:** Our representatives in government and the corporations we deal with need to know that we are paying attention. If we're silent, we're accepting the status quo. Through change we believe we can make things better for all.*

The status quo is stasis, business death. If you don't innovate, you will be left behind. This is why we make every effort to remain nimble and keep our entrepreneurial state of mind, and why we hire people who love change.

Business leaders need to learn how people respond to change, and their perception matters. Everyone perceives change through his or her own filter. What is an opportunity to one is chaos to another. A leader's role is to focus on providing clarity and communication with employees so they come to understand what the change means to them. That is precisely what we did when we announced the sale of ING Direct to our employees. We are built on a foundation of trust and transparency, and there was no question that we would share whatever we could as often and frequently as possible, to explain to our employees *why* this change is necessary.

Equipping employees with information is the single most important thing a leader can do. People don't expect only good news, so a leader must be straight, quick and direct with whatever he or she can share. And it's crucial to create a safe environment for open dialogue so employees can come to a place of understanding.

People underestimate their personal capacity for change. This is true of many other attributes too. But this is where leaders are most needed, where they can have the biggest impact. Managing change requires understanding how people perceive that change for themselves. With information, communication and trust you can help people better understand the change, so everyone can get on with accepting it, making the best of it, and seeing the opportunity within it.

An open-door policy . . . without doors

Employee engagement is one of the most important ingredients for a successful business. You can strategize about vision, innovation, collaboration and even compensation, but if your team is not "in it to win it," you have a problem.

Leaders are beginning to question years of old practices and conventional wisdom. For years, CEOs have been isolated in steel-and-glass towers, behind giant wooden desks and thick opaque doors. The fact is that CEOs, leaders and the rest of the people in an organization are the same. The challenge today is proving that humanity exists at the top, that you are accessible, that you listen, and that you want to hear from them directly. There can't be enough clarity or repetition around this message. Not when we've been trained for years to believe otherwise.

So, are you *all* in when it comes to open communication? How open is your open-door policy? How comfortable is your team in talking to you? I do not have an office. I sit at an open desk with various people and departments around me. Human Resources is to my right, our Strategy Team is to my left. No walls, doors or barriers. Anyone can drop by and chat.

The concept of ROR—return on relationships—is an important and valuable one. Enabling dialogue, being open and real, make the most difference in engagement. Recently, on Tangerine's intranet site, I asked all of our employees if there was anything about our business that they would like to bitch about. This may sound unconventional to some, but why wait for reviews and surveys to find out how your team is feeling? And will surveys actually reveal what is really being talked about at the water cooler?

These conversations are happening right now as you read this, in my company and yours. So why not find out directly what ticks off and aggravates your team during their day, and what you can do about it? Let your team in, break down the barriers and truly commit to an open-door policy, whether you take that figuratively or literally.

Getting a grasp on the true reality of your business without any filters is a huge benefit to any leader, particularly a CEO. With this you will build openness, transparency and trust. Consequently you will experience a substantial shift in the overall engagement levels of your most prized resource: your people!

Leave your office

A leader's success strongly depends on his or her ability to earn and maintain the trust of employees. So how do you build trust? You invest time in your team. You show who you really are. You get out of your office!

Business strategy is one thing, but at the end of the day it is people who drive business forward—human beings who each have their own personal reason for giving their effort and energy on a daily basis. And they want to be acknowledged, heard and valued. It's important for leaders to do that, and to genuinely care. That inclusiveness forms trust and generates immeasurable commitment towards the collective "why" of a business.

It's time to shift from a distant leadership to a more personal and engaged leadership.

The more genuine interest that leaders show their teams, the stronger the culture becomes. The impact is powerful and difficult to quantify. When you let your guard down, understand what makes individuals tick, ask about their families, truly care about their well-being—that's what makes leaders relatable. It leaves great impressions and builds great team environments, the kind of environments that foster trust and personal connections and allow for discussion, debate and even arguments at times. It builds the environments where leaders and their teams feel comfortable to show emotion and reveal who they truly are.

Connecting with people at all levels of the business in person is fundamental. There's plenty of strength in being real. It's a powerful tool, and it starts at the top. Leave your desk and get to know your teams. And if you have a chance to show your personality, do it. Engagement is an automatic result. Once the momentum is at your back it is unstoppable.

Find new ways to be transparent

It's naive to think that leaders can be 100 percent transparent. We feel the need at times to protect certain areas of our lives. So how should business leaders strike the balance?

We live in a social business era. Expectations are that we operate transparent business models, and those expectations should be supported. For the financial industry, jargon, complexity and glass towers are to be expected, right? It is a given that it, like the legal industry, is smothered in secrecy. Well, not so much. Not anymore. The pressure is on for disclosure and openness and for sharing the wealth with customers and community.

I am socially inclined; it is natural for me. Some have referred to me as the "Social CEO." Sharing stories, talking and connecting with people all come naturally. So using social media was a no-brainer for me and our organization. But there are many examples of very successful leaders who are quiet, reserved, even introverted. Which raises the question: *Is social media for everyone?* Maybe not. But the success of future leaders and their businesses may depend on their willingness to reveal who they are, who they really are, with authenticity and sincerity. Being open, sharing more about ourselves, showing a relatable side are all extremely valuable and can be real competitive advantages.

Leaders want to be seen as confident, strong and smart. We think that this is what people want from us. However, at times we feel confused, sad, frustrated and even doubtful. Hey, leaders are human too! So what happens then? Instead of trying to put your best face forward, put your *real* face forward. Redefine vulnerability as a strength. Be thoughtful how you do it, and you may appreciate how those around you grow to feel about you as a leader.

Destroy stereotypes

When you think of CEOs, you probably think of fabulous perks and grand corner offices. You might also consider the adjectives *greedy, aloof* and *egocentric*. While in some cases this perception is warranted, you should consider how much people like to glorify their role.

This is the true essence of a CEO: the inherited responsibility you have to your employees, customers, community and shareholders. Being a CEO gives you the platform to effect change, to make something happen where you didn't have the power to do so before. But this comes with great responsibility.

On my very first day as CEO, I decided to walk around and say hi to everyone. I was wearing a pair of skull-and-crossbones orange cufflinks, which I thought were very cool. However the reaction I received from one colleague was an eye-opener: "Are you here to rape and pillage everyone?" Those were her exact words. Almost five years later, we laugh about that encounter. I appreciated her honesty, but I quickly realized that no matter your personality, or fashion sense, people's natural reaction to the presence of a CEO is often anxiety.

Striking fear was not the way I wanted to lead. So what became of most importance was building trust. And of course breaking down those previously mentioned stereotypes. I do not have an office, nor does anyone else in our company. There are no walls and anyone can pass by and say hello. I often sit in the call centre and take customer calls, I park where there is a spot available, and I really enjoy having lunch with whoever is in our employee restaurant.

At the office, we are all associates. We lead without titles: you won't find titles on our business cards. We have fostered a culture that mirrors who we are as a business. How we act on the outside is exactly who we are on the inside. We are transparent, honest and approachable, and we speak in a language that people can understand. This is the future of business.

The typical stereotype of a CEO will continue to make headlines. But as the world changes we need to document better examples and inspire other leaders to take themselves off their pedestals, break down the barriers and tip the scale in the other direction. Whether CEOs are born or made is of little significance. You are only measured by the responsibility, honesty and integrity with which you lead.

Answer the phone

No two CEOs spend their days alike. Some take meetings, fly in private jets and hobnob in fine restaurants. Others come to work in jeans and spend their days haggling over lease agreements. No right, no wrong, just different approaches toward the same goal: success.

Your day-to-day approach has a big impact on you and the world around you. I spend my day in a number of different ways. Meetings, discussing marketing plans—I carve out a lot of time in my schedule for these things because they give me a chance to learn from our people and stay connected to the business.

If you polled the most driven CEOs in the world about the best use of their time, all would agree that you can never carve out too much time to talk with your two most important groups of people: your employees and your clients. Someone taught me this early on in our career, something to remember every day.

I make a point of talking to clients nearly every day, but often in a place where they look for answers: our call centre. Thousands of our clients call us daily looking for help with setting up accounts or moving money around, and sometimes they actually hear from me on the other end of the phone. How un-CEO, you say? It's the opposite. Making time every day to respond to customer emails and tweets, and routinely meeting clients in our Cafés to chat, connects me with clients in a way expensive lunches never could.

At the end of a call, hearing that a client figured out a way to pay off student debt, got advice on how to set up an account for a newborn, or now has a different perspective on retirement savings tells me not only that we are reaching clients, but that our business is making a difference and is functioning like it's supposed to.

Business intelligence comes from a lot of different places. The best comes first-hand from clients themselves. I'd never know that if I didn't take the time to pick up the phone.

Have a voice

Sixty-four percent of CEOs at the world's 50 largest organizations don't use social media. I am part of the 36 percent who do.

I can't tell you how often I am asked about why I actively participate on Twitter and Facebook. The simple answer is: why not? Sure, it's always much easier not to do something, and many organizations shy away from what could be perceived as a PR risk. But Twitter and social media are nothing new. Twitter in its simplest form is just a dialogue, a form of engagement. It is a community of individuals who are interested in the common cause of removing barriers and adding value to their lives through communication and idea exchange. That's not very different from who we are as a company. Our brand has been built on connection, engagement and word-of-mouth.

The behaviour of a small handful of irresponsible leaders over the last two decades has hurt the overall trust level that society has with corporations. People feel nothing in common with corporate interests, often seen as at odds with their local communities.

I'm a CEO of a bank, but I am also a regular guy. Much like someone picking up the newspaper or turning on the radio or television, I turn to Twitter for news, insights, sharing and inspiration. If you get past the technology or platform, Twitter is much like a community centre or a local café where conversations take place, ideas are shared and learning is achieved. I personally enjoy all sorts of dialogue, whether it is on the phone, in meetings or on Twitter. It is in my nature to be social. And so for me, this is natural and simple and fun!

Understandably, people are curious how someone in my role finds the time to be so socially engaged. My answer is that connection is a priority. I spend over 50 percent of my time connecting in various forms because it is absolutely crucial to our business. I hold the key to my Twitter account; I share insights from our business, and read and retweet other ideas that I find inspirational. Ultimately, my Twitter activities instill trust internally for our employees and externally for our customers. It may not be what our customers normally expect, but Tangerine has never bought into the status quo.

While social media is not new, emerging platforms for dialogue are putting pressure on organizations to commit to transparency and accessibility. Social media create credibility and confidence but they are not a popularity contest. They are not about being cool or innovative, or engaging in the debate of whether you're supposed to be a twitterer or tweeter. They require authenticity, contributing and sharing what is of value.

Let employees decide direction

What does it take to be an effective leader? How do we cultivate leadership? The search to identify the characteristics or qualities of leadership has been ongoing for centuries. What's remarkable is the evolution of leadership philosophies and how they're applied today. The bottom line is, we can all lead.

There is a fantastic movie, *Remember the Titans*, about the struggles of a high school football team. In one scene, the captain and assistant captain of the Titans are passionately discussing the contributions of the players to the team's success. The captain expresses frustration with the team's achievement, which drives the assistant captain to say, "Attitude reflects leadership."

Years ago, I was a lawyer. That changed when, while waiting at an auto repair shop, I struck up a conversation with Arkadi Kuhlmann. He spoke passionately about his plan to build a new kind of bank that would help people save more and borrow less. It would foster a culture where every employee and their opinions mattered, their ideas would be listened to, and some even implemented. His vision to change the way banking was done was bold and clear.

I was incredibly moved and inspired to be part of his team that would be a direct reflection of his attitude and leadership. So 17 years ago, I left my law career and embarked on a journey that aligned entirely with my own values.

Today, as the CEO of Tangerine, I come across many discussions about the struggles that organizations have regarding the attraction and retention of employees. There are varying opinions on whether money is a primary factor. You can't buy the motivations of employees. We have to recognize that there are no better motivators than allowing your employees to own the direction of your business. One of our development programs provides the opportunity for high-potential, ambitious individuals from varying departments to work closely with me, developing strategies, looking at the business as a whole and working on cross-functional teams.

Individuals who show a high level of motivation and passion and a desire to do more will do a much better job in driving a shared vision than if I just tell them what to do. All they need is an environment that promotes that type of freedom.

Entrepreneurial behaviour is crucial in the increasingly competitive environment companies face today. You want to empower your employees to own the organization's vision and execute through inspiration. We *all* have the ability to lead. We may have different leadership styles, but ultimately our passion, our self-awareness and a sense of purpose are common threads that are reflected in the many faces of leadership.

Leadership, We first.

If pride got out of the way

I've worked with many people over the years. I've seen some wonderful successes, terrible disappointments and wonderful successes that turned into terrible disappointments. Everyone has a potential that they can achieve. If the circumstances are good, we all have a shot at achieving everything we ever could—growth, progress and elevating ourselves to the next level—but how do we get there?

The only way to reach the next level is to stretch. If you want to find out how far you can go, what you can achieve, that is the only way to do it. You know this. And you also know that stretching will often lead to failure.

Many people are not much interested in stretching or achieving their potential. This is their choice and I respect it immensely. But for those who do, what stops us? Fear? Of course, but there's also pride. If pride got out of the way, what might we do, what might we try? If pride were not a human feeling, what would life look like?

- We would take more risks.

- We would stretch farther and more often.

- We would try something new.

- We would get out of our comfort zone.

- We would soar.

- If whatever we take on does not work out we would learn and not be embarrassed.

- We would move on.

- If we started a venture we believed in and it didn't go as planned, we would not feel defeated but instead take the learning for the next venture.

- If we took on a job that was too big or too tough and we did not succeed, we'd be willing to say, "I tried." And if the option were available, we would step back into another role within the same organization rather than leave to save face.

But pride often gets in the way.

Pride would rather have us leave. It makes us feel defeated and embarrassed. Pride halts our progress. What a shame. We should make it a habit to reward people who try, the risk takers, those who are willing to challenge their status quo, and we should protect those who agree to stretch too far. Let the measure of success be defined by our attempts to try rather than by the deceptive mediocrity of comfort and stability.

If pride got out of the way, we would quantify our success much the same way sixteenth-century French essayist Michel de Montaigne did: "I do not care so much what I am to others as I care what I am to myself."

The simple formula for leading people

Leading others is complex; people have different filters, different perceptions and different expectations. Is there a formula for leadership? Of course not—much like not having a magic pill to get healthy and fit, a formula or a single expert does not exist. Even the totality of all of the books ever written can't tell you how to solve the complex phenomenon of leading human beings.

So what can you do? How about starting with asking the individuals you hope to provide leadership to?

We must appreciate that we "leaders" can't get the answer right. We can only do our best without the full spectrum of information, because we simply can't get the full picture. Which is why building trust with the people you lead is absolutely crucial. Because as frequently as things change, the underlying issue of how we interpret change does not. And that insight can only come from each person you are attempting to influence, inspire and advise.

So, discuss their goals, desires and plans regularly. Give them the feedback, data and perception of others that they will need to understand how they're doing and how to get better. And ask them what *they* see, what *they* think, and most importantly, how you can best help *them*.

This is where open, honest and trusting discussions are needed, and where perspective becomes useful. Perspective offers a wide range of tools to apply to different situations. With perspective we can see the broader common trends in the data we are obtaining about someone we are leading, and we can help them focus on the wider, bigger issues without getting lost in the details of the situation.

Leading people is tough, but leadership is not about having all the answers. Leadership is a responsibility to elicit—and help people discover—the greatness they already possess.

Mentorship is a vital leadership skill

Few successful people reach their goals alone. We all need someone to guide us. This is very true of my life, which has been greatly influenced by family and mentors who shaped my professional career. Mentorship is a responsibility and a gift. And it ought to be an essential leadership skill.

Leaders must be clear about one thing—that when they are leading an organization, they are leading people. People with dreams, aspirations, ideas, expectations and fears. People who you hope want to grow and become more effective in their careers. And you should help them do just that—develop the next generation of leaders. What a legacy that is!

One of the best organizational outcomes of mentorship is creating a culture of learning that establishes the knowledge, skills, values and behaviours that produce engaged employees who can reach their full potential.

Some of my proudest moments as a leader were when I have asked our leaders to take on roles they never thought they'd succeed at, only to witness them exceed all expectations—mine, others' and most importantly, their own. That is what mentorship does. It allows the people being mentored to stretch beyond their comfort zone, to see a side of themselves they never thought they had. And it most certainly influences others within an organization to want to learn more, explore more and take thoughtful risks. I've seen firsthand how critical mentorship can be to an individual's professional advancement—most certainly to mine, and that of so many I know.

But mentorship is not solely the leader's responsibility. We all must understand how essential it is to surround ourselves with individuals who are already where we want to be and proactively seek them out. Not just one mentor, and not just within one business, but multiple people in various roles and industries who can provide a well-rounded perspective. The reality is that we all change and evolve over time. What you need from someone today may not be the thing you need tomorrow.

So be sure to seek out those you want to emulate or learn from. Take the initiative to develop yourself not only for the position you are in now, but also for the future. There is no lack of knowledge out there, but most people choose not to ask for help.

I've come to know that in life and in work you get out what you put in. And the zeal for continuous learning may be the single most important trait you need to succeed—whether through conventional educational learning, learning from experience and certainly learning from others.

I will leave you with something I remind my colleagues and myself of all the time: Give people your time, enrich your perspective, ask for help, and don't stop learning. If you follow this advice, you will have an advantage in life and you'll reach beyond your own expectations.

The glass ceiling is real

For most of my life, I've been told that male attributes are better in business. *Be assertive. Raise your hand. Lean in!*

Well, these may work for many people, but those people are mostly men. Or women trying to act like men. Luckily for me, I've been around all sorts of successful people in my career, and many have been women—but the proportions are still way off. And over the years I've wondered why the heck is it still this way?

First of all, men and women are simply . . . different. This isn't an equality question; it's about differences.

In an effort to even the playing field at the top of organizations, we have been taught that strong leaders take more risks, they plough forward, they speak up, they know when and how to be aggressive, they go faster and make big decisions quickly, they blast through, kick ass and are courageous.

What a load of bollocks that is.

The leadership competencies I look for are found elsewhere in the dictionary. They include words like *collaboration, inspiration* and *innovation*. They contain concepts like emotional intelligence, authenticity, vulnerability and empathy.

I have worked with countless tremendous women in my career, but the fact that I am even writing about this topic makes me very uncomfortable. I feel it's a controversial and dangerous subject, and the only conclusion I can draw is that my having to write about it is proof that we are still way off the mark.

Here's an example. When Tangerine publishes a posting for a

new job, we include the "requirements" that we would like to see in a successful candidate. But not everyone, I have learned from the many conversations I've had with both women and men, sees those requirements the same way. Often, a man sees that there are five key requirements and believes he possesses three of them, he goes for it. He feels confident to raise his hand and apply. A woman who possesses four of the five attributes is less likely to apply for the role. She'll pass on the opportunity because she feels she lacks something, that she isn't ready.

Having spoken to many women about this dynamic I think that leaders fall short if they fail to understand it and acknowledge the consequences: that more men will apply for the role than women, and thus it is more likely that a man will get the job even though there are more qualified women who could do the job at least as well. Sadly, men in leadership positions tend to favour those who raise their hand (just like they did) and are eager. They are simply missing the boat.

I suspect that there are many paradigms that were built in the time when only men led organizations. They are right in front of our noses, and yet we don't see them. We have to change the system, see through these ways of doing things.

One solution could be to say, "Hey, ladies, step up! Raise your hand! Take what you deserve!" But this is the male way. If leaders truly want their businesses to be great, they need to understand both genders. They need to show interest in who they are, how they work and how they perceive the world. They need to create new, unbiased processes.

The truth is that I don't get this right quite yet, and it upsets me. I'm working on it. At some point I'm going to get it right, but I could really use a hand. Diversity helps you, your team and your business gather broader views and perspectives, which helps to combat out-dated paradigms and the many biases that shape how we perceive the world around us.

Three great women have been very helpful to me over the years. My long-time work colleagues Brenda Rideout and Natasha Mascarenhas have been two of my mentors on the subject. I also had the opportunity to spend some time with Arianna Huffington recently. I asked her what advice she could give me to help me get this right. She told me that men are more likely to feel that they are entitled to "sit at the table" and many women do not feel the same. She said, "Peter, be aware that this is sometimes happening and that a little encouragement can be so powerful to ensure you are getting the benefit of all of the perspectives in the room."

ACKNOWLEDGEMENTS

I studied psychology in school and truly enjoyed learning about people and why we are the way we are. When I was younger, I whole-heartedly believed in John Locke's perspective that we are all blank slates and that our environment determines who we will become. Since having children of my own, I appreciate how nature or genetics has an impact on who we become. I believe that our nature forms the vessel that we are and that our environment and experiences fill up the vessel over time.

I must acknowledge thousands of people for contributing to who I am today, from friends and teachers to work and life teammates—and, of course, family. I am who I am because of the wonderfulness of most but also the not-so-wonderfulness of a few. I think we all need to acknowledge both constituents.

That being said, I wish to mention a few of the wonderful group specifically. My wife, Sylvia; my children, Rachel, Matthew and Ryan; and my brother, Michael. My wife's father and my stepfather, Mel, who showed me the power and beauty of what being part of a family is all about. Aline Badr—if not for her, I would not have been inspired to write this book. Justin Kingsley, my co-author, and his industrious colleague Guinness Rider. Arkadi Kuhlmann, the man who gave me a chance so long ago. He made a bet on me and showed me the power of purpose, passion and people.

Thank you to Renee, my firecracker mother, whom I enjoy making proud whenever possible. A friend once told me how special it is that my mother comes to so many of my "moments." He told me that his mother had done the same until she passed away. He asked that I continue to enjoy making my mother happy and proud.

Thank you all for filling my vessel!